DANGER ZONES

DANGER ZONES

Homosexuality,

National Identity,

and

Mexican Culture

Claudia Schaefer

The University

of Arizona Press

Tucson

The University of Arizona Press
© 1996 Arizona Board of Regents
All rights reserved
∞ This book is printed on acid-free, archival-quality paper.
Manufactured in the United States of America
01 00 99 98 97 96 6 5 4 3 2 1
Library of Congress Cataloging-in-Publication Data
Schaefer, Claudia, 1949–
Danger zones : homosexuality, national identity, and Mexican
culture / Claudia Schaefer.
p.   cm.
Includes bibliographical references (p.   ) and index.
ISBN 0-8165-1667-7 (cloth : acid-free paper). — ISBN
0-8165-1666-9 (pbk. : acid-free paper)
1. Mexican fiction — 20th century — History and criticism.
2. Homosexuality in literature.   3. Gender identity in literature.
4. Literature and society — Mexico.   I. Title.
PQ7203.S44   1996
863 — dc20   96-4484
CIP

British Library Cataloguing-in-Publication Data
A catalogue record for this book is available from the British Library.

Publication of this book is made possible in part by the proceeds of a
permanent endowment created with the assistance of a Challenge Grant
from the National Endowment for the Humanities, a federal agency.

CONTENTS

Acknowledgments

Many have contributed in a variety of ways to the completion of this volume, in manners both academic and personal (and sometimes both). Among those who have offered generous support of my work throughout the years has been Yvette Miller at Latin American Literary Review Press and *Latin American Literary Review.* The readers' acceptance, and the journal's subsequent publication, of my article on Zapata and Calva were moments of pleasant surprise and a definite source of professional encouragement. Even as recently as the late 1980s, when very little if anything was being published on gay and lesbian writing in Hispanic cultures, this journal was willing to include for its readers an article on the decidedly alternative utopian visions of these two Mexican writers. In similar fashion, Feministas Unidas has provided, and continues to provide, an open forum for the exchange of ideas on issues related to gender and to gay and lesbian writing; I would like to thank that organization for the chance to present a paper on *Dos mujeres* at the MLA meeting in 1991. The audience's response was much more enthusiastic than I ever expected, and it opened my eyes to the large number of graduate students in this country who are working on dissertations in the area of Latin American film and representations of homosexuality.

My "Other Bodies" class, an experimental course offered in the spring of 1994, introduced me to one of the most challenging and stimulating groups of students I have ever worked with at the University of Rochester. Their readings, not uniformly positive but always careful, of some of the texts treated in these essays, made me think not just twice but five and six times about the possibilities (and promises) they offer the reader. Indeed, it was the examination of broken promises that made for the liveliest debates in class. Although it is difficult to single out a handful of individuals from among so many challenging students, I would like to mention Jocelyn Janaitis, Pia Smal, and Ramón Rivera-Servera as three sources of inspiration from that special group. Their insights into complex cross-cultural issues, and their insistence on looking at texts from a variety of angles, have been a breath of fresh air, both inside and outside of the classroom.

I am grateful to *Latin American Literary Review* for granting me permission to reprint my article on Calva and Zapata, which appeared in that journal in 1989 in slightly different form. The University of Minnesota Press was equally generous with my request regarding "Monobodies, Antibodies, and the Body Politic: Sara Levi Calderón's *Dos mujeres*," which appeared in an earlier version in *Bodies and Biases: Representations of Sexualities in Hispanic Literatures and Cultures,* a volume edited by David Foster and Roberto Reis (1995).

I would like to gratefully acknowledge the support of Joanne O'Hare at the University of Arizona Press, whose interest in this project, along with a phone call or two (or three) to keep up with its progress, would serve as great encouragement for any author to complete a manuscript. The Press's readers likewise provided incisive and detailed comments on the contents of these essays, all of which contributed to the sharpening of their focus on the issues of gender and culture. Their helpful suggestions, like those of my students, made each return trip to the manuscript a journey down a familiar road with a new pair of eyes.

I am indebted to Raúl and Sixto, the brothers Rodríguez, for generously sharing their time, resources, memories, and extensive knowledge of cafés, and for proving that distance does not cut the strings of the heart.

Last, but far from least, this book is dedicated to Michael and César, whose lives had no direct connection to the project, but whose deaths came to close the final chapter.

DANGER ZONES

Introduction:

The Long

and

Winding Road

As the federal highway connecting Mexico City and Puebla snakes its way through the mountains of the Sierra Madre Oriental range in the heart of the Mexican countryside, the impending hazard of a particularly perilous curve or precipitous drop, a space to be reckoned with for its threat to a vehicle's brakes and therefore its capacity to stop at will, is announced by the appearance of the warning: "Zona de peligro." Danger Zone. Though usually the cautious motorist slows down and obeys without giving the advice any further thought, one might just be tempted not to heed the screaming yellow road sign, instead choosing to experience the consequences. Still, the prospect of some (unknown) degree of risk causes a momentary hesitation, the flutter of a heartbeat in anticipation, a more secure grasp on the gear shift or steering wheel to "keep things under control" even as one hurtles forward into unknown terrain. And if one were to do just this — throw caution to the wind and seek the thrill of transgressing the visible written mandate of the law — what would be the result? A traffic ticket from the appropriate agent of enforcement? A vivid test of one's will, or of the limits of a rental car? An unforgettable life or death experience? A so-called tragic end as the price for failing to heed the wisdom of those who have gone before? The knowledge is there for the taking.

To conjure up the appearance of the road markers set out for travelers through the maze of a society's superhighways, toll roads, and backroads alike is to put the reader on alert for any obstacles, impediments, or risks to the puta-tively methodical and reasoned completion of the (here, textual) journey. As if to break only momentarily the inertia of a body set in motion to the rhythm of the surrounding traffic made up of other human bodies, and thereby prevent the congestion caused by individual curiosity or interest, the sign is meant to warn off, keep at a distance, dissuade from closer examination, put on guard. But it also represents the ambiguity of power, for were it not for the suggestion of one's freedom to deal with the circumstances according to inclination or desire, there would be no use for the regulating tactic of the sign. The "danger" is not always quite so universally obvious, not constantly "clear and present," but it has been adjudicated beforehand by those social forces that wish to keep things flowing smoothly, in the right direction, along the straight and narrow, as a domain to be separated, circumscribed, and singled out. All manner of harm or injury is the implicit risk for those who trespass into these dominions.

The "zones" under consideration here are not necessarily to be understood only as contingencies external to the voyager, however. In fact, the aspects of affect, fantasy, stimulus, desire, and attraction left unexplored within the com-plexities of one's own identity might be viewed in remarkably similar terms, as zones purportedly better left by the roadside in the race toward some stream-lined concept of sexuality and homogeneous cultural identity. All identities, as Stuart Hall reminds us in succinct terms, "come from somewhere, have histo-ries, . . . undergo constant transformation, . . . [and] are subject to the continu-ous 'play' of history, culture, and power. Far from being grounded in a mere 'recovery' of the past, which is waiting to be found, and which, when found, will secure our sense of ourselves into eternity, identities are the names we give to the different ways we are positioned by, and position ourselves within, the narratives of the past" (1990, 225). Thus, one would in theory require the assistance of a permanent and numerous road crew to deal with the constant shifts and regroupings of such zones and division markers. What is one mo-ment's (or person's) "danger" is another's pleasure; what once may be viewed as demanding censure subsequently becomes a "zona de tolerancia" or space of carefully monitored free play and difference.[1]

This does not mean to suggest that such "zones" are somehow separate and distanced from the rest of society — an absurd notion at best — but rather that the official enforcement of a separation frequently functions to create and per-petuate the illusion that there really is one. This leads to the "dangers" being invoked in a different sense as well: as a repeated ceremonial incantation (complete with flashing strobe lights) to hide the fact that there are, as José Joaquín Blanco's phrase suggests, "uncontrollable enemies . . . within [society's] own ranks and [that] we sometimes join in challenging its basic institutions" (1991, 291). Such a manipulation of social relations and identities into Manichean realities evokes the image of the ubiquitous street hustler. While the unsuspecting observer is desperately (but confidently) looking for the money under one shell, a sleight-of-hand trick has already allowed it to be palmed and placed elsewhere. Now you see it, now you don't.[2] And while the distinguishing zones of tolerance and danger are purported to have the best interest of the public at heart, they mask the diversity of human desires within and among all facets of everyday life and in a multiplicity of forms. The process of marking and suppression therefore corresponds to what Guy Hocquenghem calls "an interpretive delusion," which leads to a constant search for signs of a homosexual threat to some ahistorical notion of a cohesive and "healthy" society, and to "a spontaneous sexualisation of all relationships with a homosexual" (55).

Similar negotiations of identity have appeared in narratives over the last thirty years of Mexican history, declarations or denials by publishers, critics, or readers to the contrary. In a variety of texts, representations of sexual identities, homoerotic encounters (real or imagined), and the individual's place in the schema of the so-called national agenda have repeatedly shifted focus as desire has been lived and experienced across ever-changing social and historical circumstances. It may come as no surprise that little attention has been given to these narrators and their tales in academic circles — particularly in Mexico, but in other Spanish-speaking countries and the United States as well — whether the reason be a perceived threat of danger to the "innocent" eye of the reader, the inaccessibility of the texts themselves, a lack of awareness on the part of readers with a potential interest in the stories told, or the relative scarcity of English translations. In any case, the result is an uneven mixture of promotion and repression, publication and subsequent relegation to dusty back rooms of booksellers' stalls or to the jumble of magazines, crossword puzzle books, pornographic pictures, and tabloid newspapers in street kiosks. And the situation for a variety of readers is complicated by the fact that along with the issue of linguistic difference — even among Hispanic cultures — these texts must also be analyzed within a context of cultural difference(s) not always evident or immediately comprehensible to an audience whose roots lie in other traditions, cultures, and socioeconomic classes. The object of critical inquiry, then, must be to attempt a series of conditional responses to what Paul Julian Smith posits as a fundamental question: "What work does [each text] do in the specific context in which it is deployed?" (15). As Mexico moves forward at top speed on the rocky and increasingly violent road leading toward the twenty-first century, this closing decade of the twentieth seems an appropriate time to take a glance in the rearview mirror before objects do indeed appear farther away than they really are (pace Baudrillard).

A principal concern of the six essays that make up this volume is the critical examination of particular narrative moments as they come into view along the routes traced by "pioneering" cultural cartographers between 1964 and 1994. The dates are not arbitrary but rather indicative of an era of transition in modern Mexican society from a more closed and protective concept of national identity to a so-called democratic integration into the New World Order, a process heralded as universally appealing to *all* Mexicans (as former president Carlos Salinas de Gortari reiterated in almost all of his public addresses).[3] How the relationships between danger and tolerance are cast in a number of texts, not as modulated and rhythmic steps in some smooth evolutionary process leading from a supposedly absolute order of prohibition to an equally apocalyptic moment of tolerance (or benign neglect, as Carlos Monsiváis characterizes the "tolerant" anonymity of contemporary urban culture [71]) but as a collection of ambiguous and tense encounters, constitutes an important part of these readings. All six pieces deal with the representation of human desire in terms of what Hocquenghem calls "an unbroken and polyvocal flux" (50). As such, there is no insinuation of perfectibility—one of the guises of the deeply rooted bourgeois myth of progress and a pillar of contemporary capitalist society, alongside the liberal defense of the sacrosanct individual—but instead a seemingly endless array of possibilities envisioned by the narrative voices. So the tales oscillate back and forth, moving constantly in a dialectic between self and state, affirmation and negation, integration and resistance, sublimity and violence. The thorny challenge of representation is taken on and resolved (at least temporarily and always contingently) in a different form by each writer, and the process of making the decision often becomes part of the narrative itself as an experiment in reflexive self-examination. The diaries of Barbachano Ponce's José Toledo and Zapata's character Sebastián (*En jirones* [In shreds]), the confessional novel-within-a-novel by Levi Calderón, the tape-recorded sessions of Adonis García with his psychiatrist, and the popular (Hollywood) film format of *La hermana secreta de Angélica María* (Angélica María's secret sister), to name just a few examples, all bear witness to this impassioned search for form. There is a case to be made for a parallel between such a desire for form and expression on one front, and the corporal desires of the characters in these works on another.

The first essay is dedicated to the analysis of a novel completed in 1962 but not published until two years later, in a privately funded edition with limited circulation. Written by the author of a number of films scripts and two subsequent novels, and film critic for the newspaper *Excélsior* since 1985, *El diario de José Toledo* (The diary of José Toledo) has frequently been overlooked by critics who tend to establish the date of the first appearance of a "gay novel" in Mexico as 1979 when Luis Zapata's *Las aventuras, desventuras y sueños de Adonis García, el vampiro de la colonia Roma* (*Adonis García: A Picaresque Novel*, 1981) was published. Though the present study attempts no such judgment of beginnings or endings (given the continuum of history and desire already mentioned as its underlying theoretical premise), the vicissitudes of publication and censorship as well as the critical passage from the "traditional" 1950s to the "modern" 1960s portrayed in its pages are indeed of unqualified interest as a backdrop for the unfolding of the story of the characters José and Wenceslao. The suicide of José Toledo might be (and has been by some) reduced to a tragic, inevitable, and mysterious act of fate unless his relationship with his surroundings (family, city, job, friends, movies, entertainment) is scrutinized at some length.

The second essay, published in an earlier version in *Latin American Literary Review* in 1989, juxtaposes two utopian narratives from the late 1970s: Zapata's groundbreaking *Adonis García* (1979) and José Rafael Calva's *Utopía gay* (Gay utopia) (1983), written in 1977. The authors' perceptions of the hopes and despairs (Adonis's "adventures, misadventures, and dreams"?) of a decade in which homosexual liberation movements coincided and joined forces with a liberalizing of the political and economic spheres are played off against the unapologetic hustler Adonis García's self-analysis and celebration of the glitter of nightlife and the pleasures of the flesh in the innocence of pre-AIDS years. The era also informs the couple Adrián and Carlos's parodic masquerade of a heterosexual couple's wildest dreams (worst nightmares?) in *Utopía gay*. Carlos, an economist and university professor, is caught between left-wing political groups and their eventual scorn of gay causes to favor instead gains in purely economic terms and his own agenda as a gay man. Adrián, his lover, announces his pregnancy, which is neither explained away by experts in medical science nor accepted by church or state (although his mother is portrayed as a fairly understanding parent who exchanges advice with Adrián about clothing, grooming, and general appearance). The situation as presented is a pretext for a strong dose of religious parody as well as the search for a utopian society, a new Garden of Eden on Mexico's Pacific Gold Coast, for this alternative "holy family."

The advent of a more ferocious capitalist bent in the Mexican economy will be a watershed to be reckoned with from this time on, as witnessed by José Joaquín Blanco's latest novel, *Mátame y verás* (Just kill me and you'll see) (1994). (That text will be the object of closer analysis in the last essay of the collection.) The 1979 winner of the prestigious Grijalbo literary prize in spite of a plethora of rabidly adverse commentaries in the press, Zapata's novel *Adonis García* went on to become a best-seller although academics and critics on both sides of the border continue to omit the text from most discussions of contemporary Mexican narrative. The mere two-year difference between the original Spanish-language version and the English translation is a credit to the efforts of Gay Sunshine Press, especially editor Winston Leyland and superb translator Edward A. Lacey, and its project of disseminating writings from other cultures to an English-speaking audience. The paradox is the novel's continued marginalization from courses on "mainstream" Mexican literature, alongside its status as an almost canonical work by other gay writers. An additional note of interest is Calva's recent admission that he has done a rewrite of his 1983 novel's utopian ending and intends to publish the new version — one for the 1990s — in the near future.

The third essay addresses Calva's 1985 novella *El jinete azul* (The blue horseman/The knight on the blue horse), a work virtually ignored by the critical establishment in Mexico and abroad, ostensibly owing to its treatment of the taboo subculture of sadomasochism. The essay discusses the concept of anthropophagy both as a personal aesthetic of cultural and sexual resistance and as a basis for measuring contemporary society's capacity to devour its own members. Published during the era in which the first acknowledged cases of AIDS appeared in Mexico, this text problematizes the issues involved in representing the margins of the marginalized, the lives and stories of those members of "modern" society situated in the shadows of a community already demonized by the official voices of so-called mainstream Mexico. As the "danger zones" of the 1960s have turned into the tolerated "lifestyles" of the 1980s, this novella heralds the ease with which intolerance and old suspicions have crept back into social discourse. An added dimension of this first-person narrator is the fact that he lives in virtual exile—from his native culture as well as from the surrounding community in the United States. A secretive resident of New York City's Forty-second Street, the surgeon-turned-stalker/natural healer narrates his journey away from medicine and its curative promises toward a reencounter with the most intense experiences of the human body and the restorative powers of remedies from the "natural world."

Essay four examines the phenomenal economic success of the Mexican bestseller *Dos mujeres* (1990), particularly among readers outside Mexico, and the swiftness of its translation into English by the author herself. *The Two Mujeres* (1991) is viewed here in the light of Mexico's official national project of "modernity" as seen through the language of recent speeches by then-president Salinas, the cultural criticism of Carlos Monsiváis, the exporting of an image of a "New" Mexico to prepare the country's entry into the "First World," and in particular the myth of "tolerance" as it relates to the free trade of images circulated under the recently implemented NAFTA (North American Free Trade Agreement). This lyrical narrative of a woman's "coming out" in middle age to her upper-class family is placed within the context of this ambiguous new vision of the Mexican state and its constitutive social body. Just how does a lesbian member of the Jewish community in exile forge an identity for herself within the current discourses on nationalism and tradition? How this novel has managed to find its way into all major Mexico City bookstores, in spite of familial attempts (by the author's father) to remove it from public circulation by purchasing all extant copies, is pertinent to this discussion as well.

The fifth essay looks at the role of popular culture, especially in commercial films, in the construction of social norms of "masculine" and "feminine" identities. Viewing the popular as a promising site of contention, this essay studies androgynous Alvaro/aspiring nightclub singer Alba María/transsexual Alexina as the three narrative voices of a single—and singular—character. The pastiche of gender identity created by Zapata in *La hermana secreta de Angélica María* (Angélica María's secret sister) demythifies the sources from which these identities are culled, as well as the perception of any polarized divisions among them. Beginning with his/her profoundly felt need to be a mirror image of 1960s bubblegum teen movie idol Angélica María, the embodiment of Mexican society's youthful feminine ideal at that time and now in the 1990s a middle-aged soap opera heroine enjoying a revival on the small screen, Alvaro traces the steps by which s/he finally reaches the unavoidable decision to become Alexina. This "mujer de lava y fuego" (woman of lava and fire) incorporates in her voluptuously sculpted figure—thanks to the modern technologies of plastic surgery—a perfect union of the physical attributes desired by the male audience in its object of adoration. (It may be noted that the real-life Angélica María bears no resemblance whatsoever to Alexina's ageless perfection.) Zapata's return to the myths of the 1960s, his inspiration in images culled from Hollywood cinematic imports, produces a textual parody that is pure kitsch. The order of the day is a consumer culture turned back by a "nationalist" Mexican society of thirty years ago but welcomed into the bosom of the national family over the past decade. A variety of questions regarding such aspects of individual and collective identities form the cornerstones of this analysis.

The sixth essay closes the volume, if only conditionally, with an exploration of three works by José Joaquín Blanco, an accomplished *cronista*, or chronicler of daily life in contemporary Mexico City, as well as a novelist with a substantial number of popular books to his credit. Blanco's influential essay entitled "Ojos que da pánico soñar" ("Eyes I Dare Not Meet in Dreams") is considered here in terms of its cautionary tone interjected into the years of *destape* (awakening, coming out, a social and cultural explosion) during the 1970s as that decade of "liberation" comes to a close. It is this essay that broaches for the first time the subject of democratic tolerance as a discursive ploy by the (wily and seductive) agents of the state to disarm and detour the projects of the seventies. Radical difference, until then a daily necessity of life for many in the gay communities of Mexico, was placed on the verge of becoming something of the past. The offer, the olive branch, in place of such a political stand, is official integration into the economic dream of the middle classes, which were willing to turn a blind eye to difference as long as there was sufficient buying power involved. (The dilemma is reminiscent of Carlos's in *Utopía gay*.) From this juncture to the publication of *Las púberes canéforas* (The pubescent nymphs) in 1983 is only a short haul. The danger that was only a potentiality on the horizon in 1979 is represented by Blanco in this later text as a fait accompli, a facet of daily life in the big city at the beginning of the years of disenchantment of the 1980s. Aside from the personal stories of a variety of urban characters, this narrative offers the reader a critical debate about choices to be made by individuals in a society that has reached a social and economic crossroads: turn left or take a right? Identity politics or a collective political agenda? Rebellion in the streets or subjects of literary discourse? The choices are difficult and hardly unanimously selected. The alternatives given in the text imply a point of radical departure on the one hand, or a comfort zone on the other. To end, if not to effect closure on, this study I turn to Blanco's latest novel, *Mátame y verás,* which presents in satiric form the utopia/dystopia of the integrated homosexual in the Mexico of the 1990s. The peculiar irony is the text's narration by a purportedly straight representative of all that has seduced the character Juanito, who is cast as the "errant" cell in the social body while Sergio is made out to be an exemplary member of "modern" society for whom the roof has just caved in.

None of the texts examined in this volume has been nor should be understood as "representative" in any general sense of an individual or group identity at any particular moment. Rather, each work has been situated in its cultural context in an attempt to establish a dialogue between (and among) the possibilities of representation and the actual components of the narratives we have before us. They all do, however, inhabit that zone we can and must refer to as Mexican culture in all its variety and mutations across the historical spectrum. In this sense, terms of spatialization—physical realities or symbolic concepts—such as "outside," "inside," "margins," or "limbo" are used here within the figurative bounds of cultural space and the power of culture to affect the construction of both individual and collective identities. The spatial locations inhabited and frequented by characters are physical presences in a geographic sense, but they are also imbued with symbolic meaning that is fluid and changes over time. And symbolic meaning often contradicts geography. Mexico City's Zona Rosa (Pink Zone), for instance, was constructed by the government with international tourism in mind, yet over the past three decades it has come to signify a much more complex relationship of constraint and liberation, limitation and self-expression. The same might be said of Cuernavaca, Acapulco, and other actual locations that, in the case of Zapata's or Blanco's characters at least, begin as contradictory spaces of periphery or marginality (invisibility) and then turn into ("come out" as?) spaces of centrality as their inhabitants have accommodated to the economic development of the past thirty years. A locus of confinement can become one of leisure and recreation recognized by the rest of (Mexican) society; yet the sense of "confinement" may continue, since they are still areas set aside for such freedom of activity. (One might consider the International Gay and Lesbian Association gatherings in Acapulco or Guadalajara as symbols of liberal acceptance or tolerance; the repression by the police over the last few years would contradict such a view, however.) The complex and frequently ambiguous relationship between symbolic and literal spaces forms an important aspect of these narratives, from the development of the middle-class "barrios" or neighborhoods of the cities in the 1950s and 1960s to the urban flight back to the provinces in the 1990s. Therefore, neither pleasure nor danger is considered an unconstrained concept, but rather one relativized within its physical and symbolic sites of practice. Perhaps, then, we should refer to these confrontations between the physical and the symbolic not so much as "liberating" zones as ones of strategic "resistance"[4] to one another.

Notes

1   I make use of a term already in existence in the narrow sense of the red-light district of a city to signify a space in which the "free expression" of sexuality (whether attached to economic reimbursement or not) is encouraged as long as it remains within the geographical confines fixed by police agencies in order to avoid the latter's overt intervention to set things "straight." This is a type of reciprocal *convenio,* or deal, in which both parties receive benefits: limited access to services for some even as they conduct on-duty patrols, tolerance for others who might otherwise be harassed economically or physically.

2   Richard Dyer refers to the same idea, this time as a generally strategic act, in his book on lesbian and gay film.

3   The government of Ernesto Zedillo Ponce de León, the party man who took over the problems left behind by Salinas de Gortari, seems to be following, at least cautiously, in his predecessor's footsteps. Political and social change, tied to increasingly harsh economic measures and the virtual destruction of the middle classes, continues to be more rhetorical than factual for many of the country's inhabitants. And accompanying drug crimes, political assassinations, and Salinas's exile is an increase in official (as well as individually sponsored and promoted) surveillance, kidnappings for ransom, and the creation of private security and police

forces whose sole allegiance is to powerful individuals such as politicians and industrialists. The protests by indigenous residents of the state of Chiapas, although nothing new in a long-term historical sense, have catalyzed the government's reliance on military force, social repression, and the use of blacklists against those social elements deemed to be in opposition to the "common goals" of the state. The surveillance aspect of this situation, in particular, does not bode well at all for guaranteeing privacy in anyone's life or freedom of expression.

4   Halperin outlines Michel Foucault's political aims in these very terms. He writes: "The goal of the struggle was not revolutionary victory so much as popular autonomy; its purpose was not to win access to state power so much as to further self-empowerment" (Halperin 56).

Works Cited

Barbachano Ponce, Miguel. *El diario de José Toledo.* Mexico City: Private edition, published in Talleres de la Librería Madero, 1964. Copyright of the author.

Blanco, José Joaquín. "Eyes I Dare Not Meet in Dreams." Trans. Edward A. Lacey. In *Gay Roots: Twenty Years of Gay Sunshine.* Ed. Winston Leyland. San Francisco: Gay Sunshine Press, 1991. 291–296.

———. *Mátame y verás.* Mexico City: Era, 1994.

———. "Ojos que da pánico soñar." In *Función de medianoche: Ensayos de literatura cotidiana.* 1979. Mexico City: Era, 1981. 181–190.

———. *Las púberes canéforas.* 1983. Mexico City: Cal y Arena, 1991.

Calva Pratt, José Rafael. *El jinete azul.* Mexico City: Katún, 1985.

———. *Utopía gay.* Mexico City: Editorial Oasis, 1983.

Dyer, Richard. *Now You See It: Studies on Lesbian and Gay Film.* London: Routledge, 1990.

Hall, Stuart. "Cultural Identity and Diaspora." In *Identity: Community, Culture, Difference.* Ed. Jonathan Rutherford. London: Lawrence and Wishart, 1990. 222–237.

Halperin, David M. *Saint = Foucault. Towards a Gay Hagiography.* New York: Oxford University Press, 1995.

Hart, Angie. "(Re)Constructing a Spanish Red-Light District: Prostitution, Space, and Power." In *Mapping Desire: Geographies of Sexualities.* Ed. David Bell and Gill Valentine. London: Routledge, 1995. 214–218.

Hocquenghem, Guy. *Homosexual Desire.* Trans. Daniella Dangoor. 1972. Durham: Duke University Press, 1993.

Levi Calderón, Sara. *Dos mujeres.* Mexico City: Editorial Diana, 1990.

———. *The Two Mujeres.* Trans. Gina Kaufer. San Francisco: Aunt Lute Books, 1991.

Monsiváis, Carlos. "Paisaje de batalla entre condones." *Nexos* 139 (julio 1989): 71–74.

Smith, Paul Julian. *Laws of Desire: Questions of Homosexuality in Spanish Writing and Film, 1960–1990.* Oxford: Oxford University Press, 1992.

Zapata, Luis. *Adonis García: A Picaresque Novel.* Trans. Edward A. Lacey. San Francisco: Gay Sunshine Press, 1981.

———. *Las aventuras, desventuras y sueños de Adonis García, el vampiro de la colonia Roma.* Mexico City: Grijalbo, 1979.

———. *En jirones.* Mexico City: Editorial Posada, 1985.

———. *La hermana secreta de Angélica María.* Mexico City: Editorial Cal y Arena, 1989.

ONE

El diario de José Toledo: The Fantasies of a Middle-Class Bureaucrat

Let them not seek to discover who I was
from all that I have done and said . . .
Only from my most imperceptible deeds
and my most covert writings—
from these alone will they understand me . . .
Later, in the more perfect society,
surely some other person created like me
will appear and act freely.
—C. Cavafy, "Hidden Things"

The peculiarly scant critical attention paid to Miguel Barbachano Ponce's 1964 novel *El diario de José Toledo* (The diary of José Toledo)[1] could be ascribed to any one (or all) of a number of reasons. Among them, the categorization of the text as "la triste historia de una pasión inútil entre el protagonista y Wenceslao, inútil y gris como la vida y el ambiente de ellos mismos" (the sad tale of a useless passion between the protagonist and Wenceslao, as useless and gray as their lives and surroundings) by Schneider (84), and Foster's similar emphasis on the "futility" (57) of the strong erotic subtext contained in Toledo's diary, would seem to have relegated it to the better-forgotten annals of what has been called "the 'tragic homosexuality' genre" (Foster 58). To perform alternate readings on the text will do little to resuscitate the character José Toledo or to condone or vindicate his act of suicide that frames the story. Yet its very appearance in a private edition subsidized by the author during the turbulent decade of the 1960s signals an obvious need to reread the book that has generally been considered the first novel with homosexuality as a central theme to appear in Mexico.[2] If one accepts as true that "La literatura homosexual en México tiene tradición" (Homosexual literature in Mexico has a [long] tradition) (Schneider 83) then it is incumbent upon the conscientious reader to do exactly what conservative conventions would dismiss out of hand based on the ideological need to maintain homosexuality invisible and absent (that is, without tradition): to look critically at changing codes of representation and self-representation within the processes of social and political change in the nation. To detach the codes of the text—the diary format, the act of writing, the counterpoint between narrators, the repression of the gay community—from their more specific context, to condemn a discourse to an ahistorical realm of tragedy or morbidity (Foster 58), is to posit a divorce between this text and those that follow, as if there were indeed no history, no tradition (as Schneider points out and examines) of homosexuality in Mexico but only some type of "genre" to which they might belong regardless of circumstances. Instead of being "liberated" from its concrete conditions of production (and consumption)—in other words, erased from everyday life—gay literature must be located in shifting and frequently controversial dialogue with the dominant culture. To dismiss any manifestations of homosexuality in literary texts other than those somehow judged to be totally "out" or unequivocally self-affirming (the latter perhaps a quest of utopian proportions) is to miss the performative aspect of gender identities and to wait for some perfect moment of absolute maximum visibility.

In Paul Julian Smith's invaluable and groundbreaking discussion of peninsular Spanish culture from 1960 to 1990 he questions just such an integral concept of the self in favor of foregrounding a constant interplay between personal identity and sociocultural contingencies. With regard to the context of modern Spain, he writes that "to focus on [the] tendency towards increasing explicitness in the representation of homosexual desire would be mistaken" (16) because that would imply some type of ontology of "progress" toward the discovery of a permanent, authentic "self" independent from social and political life on the outside. A similar conclusion may be drawn in the case of Mexican literature. The fact that Barbachano Ponce has structured his text around the counterpoint between laws (the forces of social coercion; the omniscient narrator) and desire (José Toledo's diary entries) would seem to offer a constant textual reminder of the confrontation and overlapping between the personal and the political indicative of the loudest political rallying cries of the 1960s. Discourses of legality and desire feed off one another, creating constant contention and reaccommodation. How each discourse includes or censors the other, the readings and misreadings to which the act of representation itself is subject, the appropriation of the private journal as a space of fabulation and fantasy, and an overt critique of the power of the media over the preservation of a set of unchanging moral values all form what Smith refers to as "the battlefield on which history and identity play out their conflict" (45). Any discussion of the text is complicated, however, by the fact that José Toledo's diary, evidently a literary convention but a historical marker as well, was purportedly lost on October 27, 1958, and therefore can serve the function of a bridge connecting the two decades as does the interplay between society's attendant hopes and fears during that time of passage that is also a rite of passage.

Twenty-year-old José Toledo, a minor federal bureaucrat who reportedly throws himself off the roof of a building in Mexico City's Asturias development and dies shortly thereafter in a hospital of the ISSSTE (Instituto de Servicios y Seguridad Social para los Trabajadores del Estado, or Institute of Services and Social Security for Federal Government Employees), witnesses the changes of this transitional period in two ways. First, they form a backdrop against which his own relationship with Wenceslao is played out; even if he foregrounds one over the other, neither disappears. And second, his own assimilation of many of the dominant cultural codes into his private fantasies, desires, and expectations highlights much of the ambiguity of the (empty) promises of official rhetoric.

As Mexico City acquires its luster as the singular site for cultural opportunities in the country during the 1950s, this centrism extends to economic development as well. The middle classes cut any provincial ties and lose all interest in traditional national heroes, except on the most superficial performative or ritual level. As Carlos Monsiváis writes of that decade,

> Al irse perdiendo la fe en el múltiple proceso regenerador y creador de la Revolución Mexicana en los terrenos de la cultura y el arte, va emer-

giendo la complacencia burocrática: hay que seguir creyendo *pública-*
mente en la Revolución porque no tenemos otra fuente institucional
de coherencia. . . . Los cincuentas es la década del pleito perdido. La
clase media se aburre del realismo, va desprendiéndose de sus mitologías
cinematográficas, va desertando de sus costumbres . . . , se empieza a aver-
gonzar de sus gustos y predilecciones más entrañables. . . . El desplaza-
miento de credulidades se efectúa en los cincuentas entre una aparente y
vasta tranquilidad. . . . En el sexenio de Adolfo López Mateos (1958–1964)
el proceso se institucionaliza. (1486–1488)
[As faith in the complex regenerative and creative process of the Mexican
Revolution in the terrain of culture and art begins to wane, bureaucratic
complacency is emerging: one has to keep on believing *publicly* in the
Revolution because we have no other institutional source of (national)
coherence. . . . The fifties is the decade of the lost cause. The middle class
becomes bored with realism, divests itself of its cinematic myths, deserts
its customs . . . , it begins to feel ashamed of its most beloved tastes
and predilections. . . . The shift in belief is produced in the fifties amid
an apparent and vast (mood of) tranquility. . . . In the six-year term of
(President) Adolfo López Mateos (1958–1964) the process becomes insti-
tutionalized].

Such "tranquility" is, of course, exposed as a bourgeois myth of its own during the 1960s. José Toledo's diary reflects much of this false complacency and
tranquility.

A great number of intellectuals are hired to work at the service of the federal government in a variety of official functions during the 1950s and, in 1959,
when Demetrio Vallejo and other railroad union leaders and organizers are
jailed, few if any speak out on their behalf. The general feeling is that labor
and class interests belong to the past, not to modern urban Mexico, which is
keeping an eye on its international image, and that the goal to pursue at all
costs is modernity: "Modernidad no política sino social, cultural y sexual"
[Not political, but social, cultural, and sexual modernity] (Monsiváis 1491).
Commercialism is touted as the key to personal success, as witnessed in the
inauguration of the trendy Zona Rosa [Pink Zone] as a space to show off
the nation's "belonging" to modernity. Culture is the exclusive property of the
capital whose innate right to this label is promoted through the recently en-
trenched mass media. One of the most accessible means of enjoying the bene-

fits of this modernity is the movie theater, a preferred locus of activity for José Toledo and his friends and co-workers, who frequent the numerous downtown cinemas in search of companionship, romance, and strong doses of what are considered films of Mexico's "Golden Age" as well as an equal or greater number of foreign (mostly U.S.) imports.[3] A succession of political repressions and assassinations between 1958 and 1968 are tolerated by the "apparently tranquil" middle classes as the price to pay for moving ahead with the project of development, a blindness exhibited by Toledo in the case of the "maestros normalistas" [grade- and secondary-school teachers] who storm the offices of the "Secretaría" where he works (most likely the SEP or Secretariat of Public Education, the Mexican equivalent of the U.S. Department of Education) and are turned back by the police with riot gear and tear gas as Toledo tries to concentrate at his desk on writing in his diary. For him their shouts are merely annoying background noise, but one finds echoes of their inconformity in the very words of this diarist as well. The separation between inner and outer worlds is presented as incomplete (at best) and, truth be told, genuinely impossible.

Within the vision of "sexual modernity" described by Monsiváis, then, where might *El diario de José Toledo* fit? It was printed privately with funds from the author and never republished. Its complex and somewhat melodramatic (at times almost campy) characters have been, at least in the past, physically involved with each other yet they find little real space in this "sexual modernity," even if their daily lives revolve around all the *rest* of the social and economic values of development promoted by the government and the media. The city once mythified in Carlos Fuentes's novel *La región más transparente* (1958) (*Where the Air is Clear,* 1960) as the urban metropolis that "Abriga o alberga o destruye nuevos aristócratas, nuevos ricos, prostíbulos de set cinematográfico, filósofos en el vacío, toreros, homosexuales, bongoseros, peladitos, obreros, taxistas, periodistas" (shelters or harbors or destroys nouveaux aristocrats, the nouveau riche, brothels straight out of movie sets, philosophers in limbo, bullfighters, homosexuals, conga players, ragamuffins, blue-collar workers, taxi drivers, newspaper reporters) (Monsiváis 1495) simultaneously holds out a playing field of possible alternatives (in cruising the city's parks and gay bars, for instance) and violently takes them away at will. Any "tolerance" of a homosexual relationship is posited on the city's "sheltering," in Fuentes's words, of anyone and everyone; once the glue holding them all together comes apart—that is, once economic means disappear—

then the city merely "harbors" or even "destroys" those declared undesirable. While Toledo's father, for appearance's sake he says, obliges his son to stay at home one evening instead of taking off in a taxi after a miffed Wenceslao and interrogates him as to whether he "keeps" his friend in clothes and gifts (10), Wenceslao's father is willing to overlook his son's "friendship" with the other young man because this patriarch dreams only of credit cards, financial progress, and the possibility of the family's gaining such economic mobility through José Toledo. These are not two separate and distinct realities but two sides of the same coin, two attitudes or codes that coexist in often desperate contention within Mexican society in the late 1950s. They form part of the context for the diary we have before us, a document *someone* found fit to turn over to a reading public (if we play along with the authorial game to create a greater distance between a text and its source) and the ultimate portrait of a love-hate relationship between individual and society, between utopian desires and coercive laws, between the two young men.

The tale begins simply enough with the presentation of "a literary found object" (Abbott 18) that serves to contradict the official media version of events given on the first page (7). Why indeed a popular young man with a good job and lots of friends would "throw himself into the void" is a question his parents avoid answering but one to which a voice from beyond the grave will respond by means of the written words he has left behind. The discrepancies between the two documents point out from the very beginning the need to read these representations of events with great care. Through a record peppered with intermittent gaps and based on alternating moments of intense passion and crushing despair, José Toledo builds up an intricate, self-conscious version of his search to regain the object of desire he has lost, Wenceslao, after having met one year, nine months, eleven days, and fourteen hours before (62). Because we as readers are given advance notice of his death by his own hand, the suspense is different than it would be if we were unaware of the outcome. Yet rather than read the story tragically—as the tale of an intrinsically "flawed" person condemned to this and no other possible end—we can begin by looking at José Toledo as a victim of a series of misreadings by himself as well as by others. Such misreadings, perhaps most clearly resulting from the complexity of representing and deciphering signs of identity in so-called legible social codes (Garber 25), occur with great frequency in the counterpoint between the narrator and the diarist. In search of some way to express his attempt to maintain a daily routine after Wenceslao's rejection and subsequent departure for Guadalajara, Toledo turns to a diary in which he records his dreams of a reconciliation with Wenceslao, his increasingly mundane professional activities, his oppressive family life, his hopes and desires, while the alternating narrative pieces fill in what can be viewed as mainstream society's possible readings of them. The narrative ambiguities and contradictions allow for interpretation, unlike the proposed univocal reading of the obituary notice.

While Toledo addresses Wenceslao directly in his journal meant for their eyes only—a paradox since the reader is told in the first few pages that Wenceslao has ceased answering the telephone and refused to meet his friend in person, and will find out at the end of the text that the diary is eventually lost on a city bus before its intended recipient ever sees it—the narrator's remarks tend to exacerbate the distance between the two men. They also denigrate the insistence of Toledo on his feelings for Wenceslao as a willful exaggeration of "natural" affect projected into the realm of what one critic has referred to as the "fundamentally deranged" (Foster 57). One instance occurs when Toledo, in his version of the events, accompanies an older gentleman co-worker, Señor González, to the movies after much insistence on the part of the latter. The theater reminds him of Wenceslao, whom he has accompanied there many times, and his gaze roams over the audience nostalgically seeking out his friend's face (to no avail). Since he doesn't want to reveal his relationship with another man for fear of the reaction of this companion whom he hardly knows, Toledo makes up a story about searching for an ex-girlfriend to pacify the curiosity of González. Afterwards, he writes in the diary, to justify this act to himself as much as to Wenceslao, that "Como comprenderás, era necesario inventar ese cuento para que no sospechara de nuestras relaciones" (As you will undoubtedly understand, it was necessary to invent that story so that he [González] wouldn't suspect anything about our relationship) (70). (Wenceslao is also sometimes cast as a sick friend and other times as a cousin undergoing emergency surgery in José's stories to others.) But the omniscient narrator, not content to leave this "aside" to the implied reader (Wenceslao) as is, turns it into an opportunity to comment on Toledo's entry in the text as a misrepresentation, or at best a partial one, of the circumstances. By purportedly reading the mind of the enamored writer, the narrator shows us evidence that he is duplicitous and even more obsessed with Wenceslao than he seems at first glance: " 'Si no se atreve a tocarme, aprovecharé de todas maneras el hecho de que me haya convidado para relatarlo en el diario y provocar los celos de Wenceslao' pensaste" (If he doesn't dare touch me, I'll take advantage of the fact that he's invited me [and paid my way into the movies] anyway to narrate it in the diary and provoke Wenceslao's jealousy, you thought) (72). Does José repress this manipulation of the scenario to which the narrator has privileged access, or is the narrator warning the reader to beware of reading the diary too simplistically? Or is he just maliciously reading this into José's thoughts? This "hidden" dimension of José Toledo as a man who sexualizes all social situations (no matter what the real motivations or outcomes) would appear to confirm two of society's worst fears. The first is that gay men and lesbians might mingle among others without being "recognized" and therefore pose a silent (and secret) "danger" to heterosexuals as the targets of their desires, which are never completely controlled (in other words, Señor González should beware the machinations of José). And the second is that gay men and lesbians live only in a sexual dimension in which fetishes and obsessions dominate any other possible aspects of life. Such suggestions preclude the idea that José and Wenceslao might really feel a sense of loss at the end of a relationship (or even that these men *can* have an emotionally fulfilling relationship at all), or that they relate to one another in terms of possessiveness and jealousy *exactly* as the men and women around them do. This relationship of control holds true for heterosexual couples from all walks of life. We have only to look at their parents, their acquaintances Leonardo and Soraya (39–40), or Mercedes who lies awake at night incessantly repeating the litany "Amante, autoridad, dinero, edad" ([A] boyfriend, [his] control, [lots of] money, [of the right] age) (41) to find numerous examples of such behavior in which partners relate to one another in very codified ways.

   In fact, the supposed harmony and mutual support of the traditional family structure takes a beating in *El diario de José Toledo*. The values upon which it is founded, according to divisions of gender and labor, are the submission of the female (and all offspring) to the domination of the male, and the protection of this image, at least in public, at any price. One example of the institutionalized image of husband and wife can be found in Wenceslao's parents, a relationship that survives in José when he refers to Wenceslao as his husband (52). Wenceslao's mother accuses her spouse of ruining their reputation by being "grosero, vulgar, sucio" (coarse, vulgar, dirty) (26) while, by inference, she considers herself to be refined, clean, and proud. When the family goes out to dinner, the scene becomes one of a domineering woman who dresses her husband and son to her liking (for she is somehow the only one with "good taste"), then ignores both of them, considering them below her in social status, once they are out in public. Yet she later transfers her hopes for a "decent" family onto her one and only son, a role he refuses to accept because he identifies more with his father as a social "renegade" than with the orchestrated appearance of harmony and obedience promoted by his mother. Wenceslao's father is equally interested in his son's future, to the degree that it is linked to his own, but only in terms of potential financial gain from his son's friends, all of whom are acceptable as long as they are economically sound. For Wenceslao's mother, whose over-bearing image becomes the "enorme piedra blanca, carcomida e inamovible" (huge, white, rotted, immovable boulder) (11) in her son's dreams of suffoca-tion and drowning, family pride and social class cannot accept the "wrong" object of desire. She says: "José Toledo, el cine, aquel muchacho" (José Toledo, the movies, that young man) (11), referring to the two corrupting influences on her son's life. Both person and place are inappropriate; no one worthwhile would be seen in such places, and by going there one loses status. For both parents, class is the real issue here, whether in terms of appearance or actual means to belong to "modern" society. And Wenceslao acts as if he were unable to escape the dilemma or make any type of choice except to run away from all potential confrontations. The family's relatives in the province of Morelos are hardly any different. The chilling scenes of an uncle's brutal treatment of his wife (89–91) for having gone to a beauty parlor without his permission are an unforgettable dramatization of the violent tensions behind the façade of perfect role playing. The victimization of the wife whose makeup is forcibly removed and whose hairdo is destroyed under the faucet, and whose protests go unheeded — "aquí en mi casa, digo lo que se me antoje y usted se calla" (here in my house, I say whatever I please and you madam will just shut up) (90), he reminds her in no uncertain terms and in formal address — suggests a relationship of inequality, jealousy, and fragile dependence reminiscent of José Toledo and Wenceslao. The threat of the woman taking over the "domain" of the man of the family, whether exemplified by Wenceslao's mother or by the relationship between two young men (who is to play the role of the "man"?), appears to prompt the traditional family's disintegration.

The story of José's unmarried sister Socorro is yet another instance. Even if he seems oblivious to her suffering at the hands of their father when her pregnancy is revealed, the details of the story are sufficient to establish parallels with Wenceslao and José. Socorro sits by the telephone waiting for a call from the father of her child—a man to whom she submits physically when he threatens to leave her in a fit of jealousy—but it is an act of pure futility. And the parents blame each other for this family "disgrace," saying it is due to a lack of proper education on the part of their daughter. She does not know how to play her role. But José is no different. His days in the office are filled with hours of frustration when the telephone call from Wenceslao never comes, and he becomes distracted from his duties as he imagines the reasons for this, the majority of the time deciding that Wenceslao is out with other men. He calls a neighbor in Wenceslao's building on a daily basis to inquire if there is any news from his friend, only to be admonished by the family not to annoy them any more for fear of creating a public scandal. Their relationship, however it might be defined, must be kept "in the family." In the end, neither brother nor sister manages to communicate with any satisfaction: José composes a diary that the intended reader never sets eyes upon; Socorro moves back home under the protection of her father to await marriage at a future date to a man who will assume the role of her parents. José therefore should not be judged as acting in "pathetic" (Foster 58) or sentimental fashion of his own volition, because this mode is obviously the one that predominates in life and film (actually, all media)[4] and that dominates all relationships portrayed in the text regardless of the gender of the participants.

José Toledo calls Wenceslao's home, he stands on street corners in the hope that his beloved will pass by, he sends him letters that are returned unopened, and he mentally recreates the details of their previous encounters in restaurants, bars, and movie houses. Although seemingly aware of the pressures of family and society (especially social class) on them, Toledo neither denies his feelings for Wenceslao (in fact, they persist throughout the diary even if they are not discussed in so many words with friends and relatives) nor rejects the idea of his attraction toward another man. He has already "lusted" (62) after the young man Ramón, and when two other youths approach him on different occasions to declare their desire to "become friends," as such same-sex relations are disguised here, the only reason they are spurned is that José claims he must be faithful to his lover Wenceslao. On the other hand, the narrator's voice uses Alberto Paredes Salas, the second of José's admirers and the one that most reminds him of Wenceslao in appearance and demeanor, to reaffirm a stereotype of gay men in Mexico. Toledo's last lengthy entry in his diary before leaving it on the seat of the bus, and before committing suicide, recounts what *might* have taken the form of a tender portrayal of two attractive young men meeting on a bus and how their affection develops. Instead, shortly before his death, Toledo is exposed to an almost didactic sounding speech on homosexuality, which he claims he doesn't want to hear but to which he is compelled to listen. Paredes Salas tells him, and he repeats verbatim in the pages of the diary (in quotation marks), the following: " 'nosotros los que estamos en este enredo, debemos hablar claro a las personas que nos gustan. . . . Mire, joven . . . si de verdad comprende a los homosexuales debe darse cuenta de que todos somos iguales. Usted, yo o cualquier otro, al salir de excursión, haría lo mismo que está haciendo su amigo: buscar aventuras' " (those of us who are in this tangled mess, we ought to speak clearly to the people we like. . . . Look kid, . . . if you really understand homosexuals you should realize that we're all the same. You, I, or anyone else, when we go on a trip, we'd all do the same thing your friend is doing: look for adventures) (123). Up until this point, and despite what his mother calls the "habladurías de la gente" (people's gossip) (25), perhaps José Toledo *hasn't* "really understood" one important point: that a homogeneous image of homosexuals is what makes gay men and women socially invisible (even if they are economically visible as consumers), an ideology that has already filtered into Paredes Salas's self-image. José has sorted out his feelings toward Ramón and Wenceslao on an individual basis, not as two variants of a single identity: the first was the object of his lust, the second of his undying romantic love. Since José Toledo's diary has reflected his desire for a monogamous relationship throughout, and even his language echoes the most conventional dialogue between heterosexual lovers (as promoted on the movie screen in particular) with the refrains "sabes que soy tuyo en cuerpo y alma y lo seré toda mi vida" (you know I'm yours body and soul and I will be all my life) (9) and "Nunca habrá quien pueda consagrarse enteramente a ti como yo" (There will never be anyone so totally devoted to you as I am) (43) repeated at frequent intervals, he obviously doesn't conform to the image of physical adventure and promiscuity suggested by others. Following so closely on the heels of this conversation, his suicide appears infinitely more connected to the role he sees he is being forced to play than to the boy-meets-boy, boy-gets-boy, boy-loses-boy scenario. The modern metropolis is populated by anonymous masses struggling to get ahead, not by individuals.

And what of Wenceslao? As José fights constant battles with language to put his thoughts down on the blank diary page, Wenceslao remains silent. In letters, telegrams, and even the lyrics of a romantic song he dedicates to his absent love, José never seems to give up. Writing becomes his daily routine and his emotional sustenance. One Tuesday morning he arrives at the office early, puts all official work aside, and writes the following to Wenceslao: "me apresuré a escribirte. Dilaté casi tres horas en redactar la carta. Tardé tanto porque es difícil expresar los sentimientos que guardo en mi corazón" (I hurried to write to you. I spent almost three hours drafting the letter. I took so long because it's hard to express the deep sentiments I hold in my heart) (33). Yet José sends this letter, writes others, and keeps up the diary to the very end. So when the narrator tells us that the diarist doesn't manage to express himself very well, that he suffers from "la imposibilidad de racionalizar [sus] sensaciones" (the impossibility of rationalizing [his] feelings) (88) or finding the words to convey them, it just doesn't ring true. Not only does José Toledo produce a journal, but we hold a novel in our hands as well, a text perhaps imperfect but quite real in its physical presence. Wenceslao is the one who doesn't seem to find a way to express himself here, and we have no way of knowing anything about his life after Toledo's text ends. What we do learn of him comes to us through the comments of the omniscient narrator, who fills in the events of this character's life once he leaves José. But Wenceslao's presence is only secondhand.

In his flight from their relationship — and in certain measure from himself — Wenceslao is depicted in a variety of situations. He returns to a brothel to look for a prostitute he had met earlier to propose marriage (as a way to "erase" his past life with José), only to find out that she has been killed by a violent client in the meantime. He is shown frequenting a transvestite bar in a rundown Mexico City neighborhood, where he meets a ventriloquist whose cloth puppet asks if he feels alone and abandoned, a question that strikes a chord of sadness to which he responds by having sex with the ventriloquist and then asking to be paid (20). (It is revealing to point out that only a ventriloquist's dummy, a nonverbal being speaking with the voice of another, is capable of making him react so strongly.) In a lengthier narrative passage we also see Wenceslao going door-to-door in a "patio de vecindad" (slum; tenement rowhouse) begging women for their used apparel to dress in when he goes to the bars at night. Upon entering the protective environment of the private club, he takes on a different identity as a *fichera* (B-girl) and makes a meager living by collecting money for dancing with the customers. This enclosed space is presented in harsh contrast to the violence of the streets as he makes his way along the small plazas and busy thoroughfares to the nightclub. In contrast to José, Wenceslao is presented as quite aware of the imminent danger of his route, of the fact that he might be the next person chased and cornered by the chain-wielding gangs that cruise the area looking for gay men or transvestites to beat up. The brief reference to one such episode leaves the reader with few doubts as to the atmosphere of persecution on these mean streets and the scapegoating of certain members of the community. When one gang member yells to the rest "¡Ahí hay uno, agárrenlo!" (There's one, grab him!) (16), the subsequent chase is described as a pack of animals going after their prey "como lebreles excitados" (like excited greyhounds) (16). In this climate of what the narrator calls "el anárquico principio de una cruzada purificadora" (the anarchic beginning of a purifying campaign) (31), there are two fundamental targets for society to purge itself of "undesirables": political protesters such as teachers and other organized union employees in search of better working conditions; and what José's mother refers to as the socially lost or misguided, the "different" or "irregular" or "abnormal" (25) such as her gay son, who risk their lives every day by just going to work or to meet their friends, to say nothing of pursuing or even fulfilling their desires. While the street gangs demonstrate one manner of dealing with these "undesirables," society calls on the army and the police to deal with them in a more concerted fashion. And José's mother has her own remedy of sorts: trying to conjure away his "difference" by the constant repetition of words to the effect that he can be changed (cured?).

It is through his abundant dreams that the narrator has Wenceslao's subconscious reveal the tensions of his life, otherwise kept hidden. Even after borrowing money from José to flee from Mexico City—and paradoxically from the very source of this money himself—Wenceslao can't escape a feeling of entrapment and doom. This is ironic given the fact that it is José who commits suicide and not Wenceslao. Yet this portion of the narrative functions in a kind of counterpoint to the diary's almost insular obsession with lost love, which recounts little of the inner life of the diarist with the exception of his thoughts about Wenceslao. (Concern with how they are viewed by others or considerations of any concrete persecution don't really surface to a great extent at any time in Toledo's narrative segments.) The dreams tend to take the form of a solitary figure, Wenceslao himself, trapped by natural forces such as oceans, rivers, narrow dirt roads, deluges of mud, and cavernous rocks, that are filled with, or consist of, rotting debris and that surround him until he goes under or stops breathing. The most vivid example of such a figurative contamination of cleanliness, the forces of nature sullied by filth, is the dream in which Wenceslao finds on his otherwise clean pant leg a whitish blob which repulses him but which seems permanently stuck to the fabric like a leech to skin (34–35). Wenceslao fights to remove this visible mark from his clothing with more vigor than he makes decisions or takes any action on a conscious level. Perhaps this owes to the fact that in the dream he finds himself in public, accompanied by others, and the spot signals his "difference" from them, a distinction he wishes to keep hidden. When he finally manages to remove the gelatinous material, it falls to the floor at his feet, where its presence continues to threaten him as its dimensions increase to tremendous proportions and it grows tentacular appendages that reach out to engulf him in its mass.

In José's diary, their relationship is referred to as "nuestras cosas" (our things) (9), that is to say their phone calls, chats, gossip, dates, meetings, fights, physical contact, etc., and the narrator's fervent wish for it all to continue. But for Wenceslao, everything is tentative and uncertain, at least according to the narrator, who tells us that Wenceslao "no sabía con certeza si le amaba o no" (didn't know for sure whether he loved him [José] or not) (15), and instead of one swift suicidal act he proceeds to kill himself slowly with constant overdoses of alcohol. José tries to recreate the past over and over; Wenceslao tries to abolish it by drowning it in drink. Language seems to meet a dead end in both cases. For Wenceslao, avoiding any conversation with José is a priority and he has to be forced by his mother to be sociable when his friend visits their apartment. He never answers his correspondence, doesn't have any co-workers because he is unemployed, gets into heated verbal altercations with an uncle, and stalks José to see how he spends his time and with whom, but never confronts him or exchanges a word about his activities later on. On the other hand, José stagnates in the single refrain of "lo mucho que nos queremos" (how much we love each other) (9) which appears at intervals throughout the text much as the handkerchief, gold chain, and ID bracelet given to him by Wenceslao make their appearance every night in a ritual of conjuring up his lover before drifting off to sleep. One conventional device of diary writing is repetition or narrative ritual as a means of reconstructing the fragments of experience in a personally meaningful way. José fixates on his real or imagined experiences with Wenceslao as a utopian object of adoration, one onto which he projects his secret (although revealed in the diary) fantasies, most of which seem to revolve around being reunited with him forever. José never goes beyond this point, however, to envision any details of their (possible) life together. The Wenceslao of the diary is no longer the "real" Wenceslao—who will never read the diary addressed to him either—but an absolute figure frozen in time and space whose image no human being could ever live up to. José wants not to lose this last vestige of Wenceslao, his memory, since their love is unrepeatable except as pale copies of the original experience; and the only way to keep the feeling alive is to adhere to the same (original) language without variation. The precariousness of the physical relationship between José and Wenceslao is echoed in the material document itself: the diary escapes from the hands of its writer and is left behind for someone to find (here, the unidentified narrator, it is assumed) and read in order to recreate the past. Although the text of the diary is not composed originally for the eyes of anyone but its writer and Wenceslao (in theory anyway), that closed circle of communication is widened at the moment of its encounter by the eyes of the "outside" world.

The naïveté of Ramón, the young man whose body is lusted after by José as revealed in his brief written confession to Wenceslao, leads to his own death. But this is only half the story; the other half bears a lot of resemblance to the tale narrated by José. Each is youthful and attractive, each has access to money (one through his job and its benefits, the other from recent lottery winnings), each wants to enjoy life to the maximum, and each becomes the victim of his desires. José meets Wenceslao, open his heart to him, takes out exorbitant loans to satisfy the whims of his lover, and dies disillusioned by the other's refusal to play his "role" as beloved any longer. Ramón cruises the downtown Alameda Park in his car, picks up two young men, shows them a fistful of bills, and is carved up with a knife when he refuses to hand over his winnings once they reach the apartment. In his distrust of the press, José refuses to read the newspapers and goes several months without learning of Ramón's homicide. When he does, it is one of the very few moments when José feels directly threatened, because many times he has spent the night in the apartment where Ramón was killed. Each has reached the brink of happiness and expectation, and each has been turned back by the intrusion of the so-called forces of reality into the situation at hand (Wenceslao's doubts and family pressures; the greed of the young assailants). Each has become the victim of an increasingly violent and impersonal society whose members are interested in taking advantage of whoever is foolish enough to still be honest and not to create a protective image.

In other words, identity here is *only* representation, and one's public image is one's only identity. All gay men are "adventurous," as José is told by Alberto; two adolescents hiding in the back of a bus talking to one another in hushed whispers are "ambiguous," "passionate," (79) and in love as read by José. His empathetic identification with them and with what he sees as their plight as lovers, however, is labeled a misreading by the narrator who calls them just "inseparable friends" (82) who once belonged to rival gangs but have now joined forces. In a society in which the word "friend" is used by José for Wenceslao, and to refer to his two chance acquaintances as well, though, a space is created for interpretation and emotional investment where otherwise none might have existed. Such linguistic ambiguity allows for communication and survival in a city personified in the text as an immense crocodile (27) whose streets look like giant throats that devour traffic (10) and feel like molten lead (13) to those who traverse them. Such an atmosphere of violence does not permit adolescence—José is only twenty, after all, and is called "joven" (young man) by many of those he meets—to be a time of innocence and honesty, especially for someone like José Toledo who more than anything else yearns to tell everyone about his love for Wenceslao. Instead, he learns he must disguise himself and his longings. He finds out that he has recourse only to the privacy of the diary, and that he must encode the rest of his life according to such socially acceptable terms as friendship or collegiality. He also learns the hard way, when a private party he attends is raided by police who have planted informants among the guests, that money can buy innocence and tolerance from the authorities, thereby creating an unequal system of justice and social visibility for homosexuals depending on their economic means. In the long run, it becomes fairly evident that the tremendous effort made by José to pursue Wenceslao's affection, to draft a written record of his daily trials both at home and at work, and to maintain his dreams alive is no small feat. His acquaintance Alberto Paredes Salas recognizes and is drawn to these attributes, first as a sign of gullibility (123), but then as an endearing and almost outmoded type of social behavior. He tells José that "de gentes como usted cualquier extraño se enamora de inmediato. Se ve a la legua que uno le amaría toda la vida sin contratiempos ni sobresaltos, por eso, para hallar a alguien parecido es preciso buscar entre mil" (any stranger would fall in love with someone like you immediately. You can see from a mile away that one could love you for a lifetime without worries or unexpected fears, that's why finding someone like you is finding one in a million) (123–124). This might sound like just another rerun of José's declarations to Wenceslao, again confirming that "all homosexuals are the same" down to the level of affective language, but there is more to the encounter than meets the eye. What Alberto stresses between them is not a physical attraction or sentimental attachment but a "confianza" (trust, faith) (124) set up between them in their conversation, a closeness and honesty not shared by José and Wenceslao that appears in this, the last detailed and lengthy diary entry before the end of the text and the disappearance of the diarist.[5]

Without diminishing in the least the tragic act of suicide, and in fact emphasizing Ramón's bloody sacrifice as well, it seems that an argument can be made for the existence in this text of an underlying tone of nostalgia combined with a bitter warning that representation and reading are acts that carry profound, even dire, consequences for the individual, the community, and the nation. Such a word of caution is especially valuable in the 1950s and 1960s, during the rapid advances of technology and the mass media in Mexican culture, and the equally rapid growth and development of Mexico City itself as a mecca to which are drawn the hopeful dreamers from every part of the country. Monsiváis writes that there was a strong belief then, not unlike in the present, that the media should be utilized to create a society cohered around a certain set of values regarding family, consumption, and a shared sense of morality as aspects of a "modern" nation. He states that "Crear un país es teatralizarlo" (To create a nation is to depict it in masquerade; to present it in all its theatricality) (1519) for all of society's consumers to internalize; this is precisely what occurs in the newspapers, television, radio, and cinema of the time. The age of innocence is past, and the "modern" era of mechanical reproduction, not the confessional honesty and genuine "aura" of the diary, is upon us (them). José is quickly becoming an anomaly in his desire to cling to an individual rather than some unending string of lovers to be consumed just because they are there and available and, as Alberto reminds us, "all the same." (Adonis García, the protagonist of Zapata's novel mentioned at the beginning of this discussion, takes the step José Toledo rejects by choosing instead to end his life: he walks the streets of the greatest human marketplace, Mexico City, and feasts day and night on the delicacies he finds there.) All the saintly patience of the character Alberto Paredes Salas, who swears he will wait forever for José to change his mind, can't compete with the explosive encounter between this twenty-year-old chained to the federal bureaucracy and the images to which society wishes to make him conform. Only his diary lives on as inescapable testimony to his (brief) presence.[6]

José Toledo's story is a lingering one with an abrupt ending; it leaves out many details but includes innuendo of all kinds. Was José a less-than-perfect bureaucrat who didn't appreciate the opportunity of belonging to the broader consumer society through the perks of his office job among men and women who looked the other way when it came to his daydreaming, personal phone calls, and surreptitious lunch rendezvous? Or perhaps Wenceslao was unwilling to make a public commitment to a male partner (or admit his own attraction to men), yet was more than willing to accept the social and financial benefits that accrued from José's integration into the up-and-coming federal bureaucracy. While the narrative clears up some of the mystery behind the death of José, at least making it problematic, it creates a new sense of ambiguity in the process by leaving the reader with a more general question about the physical and psychological survival of an individual within the context of the modernizing metropolis.

We must not lose sight of the fact that the text before us is entitled José Toledo's diary; it is not, nor does it pretend to be, Wenceslao's confessions, whether to José or to some interested third party. The focus is squarely on this problematic member of the newly developing middle class and on his relationship to the culture that has produced the conditions of his daily life. The narrative voice, scattered among the fragments of the diary, must be identified with the finder of this testimony and therefore with the (fictional) individual who has made the decision to preserve and disseminate the story. Though castigating remarks about the naïveté of the diarist reverberate throughout, the narrator is at the very least interested in expanding both the brief newspaper obituary announcement and the single focus of José's own accounts, since both are included. Each plays off the other to compose a text filled with new silences — what is omitted from the press version can only, at best, be partially explained by the frequently plaintive monologues of José. Yet, as we have seen, his diary is in reality a dialogue in its search for self-understanding within the explosive atmosphere of the city, one in which overt sentiment is marginalized and human relationships are codified in terms of economics. In the midst of circulating wealth and available pleasures—as exemplified by the national lottery, bureaucrats' discussions of their latest sartorial acquisitions, an emphasis on disposable income to fund vacation getaways or frequent visits to the theater and the cinema, and his recognition as a steady customer at an upscale restaurant—José Toledo seems to reject, or at least not care to recognize, the road to happiness offered him by society. He sacrifices meeting friends in cafés to stay at home and await Wenceslao's return from Guadalajara, lavishes money and gifts on his object of desire, who still sees fit to leave him in the lurch, neglects his appearance, and leaves his diary on a *second-class* bus. Such details add to the complexity and ambiguity of the narrative, in whose pages the concept of resistance takes on a variety of guises. They are not all successful.

That the character José Toledo dies in the arms of the federal government, which promises its employees (children?) protection and care from the cradle to the grave, is evidence that even the most wayward child will be taken in by this surrogate parent or guardian. Basically untouched since its construction in the 1950s as a bastion of health care and family support for federal workers, the 20 de noviembre ISSSTE Hospital in the center of Mexico City remained as a monument to such government policies until the 1985 earthquake. That a suicide victim has such a place to be cared for, such a space of symbolic nurturing and support—whether reasons are given for his act or not—indicates simultaneously that José is at odds in some way or another with life in the capital *and* that there is a safety net to catch him should he fall. Unlike in the 1980s and 1990s when AIDS clinics and medical facilities for AIDS patients are often the targets of social censure and acts of violence, at least some part of José's collective family is willing to recover the body and the story of one of its own.

While retaining the gambit of distancing the author from the literary creation, the lost diary device allows for speculation on the identity of the narrator into whose voice the story has been displaced by the silencing of José's own. Might it be one, or both, of the adolescents overheard by José on the same bus shortly before, those with whom he feels a kinship through their intimate whispers? Is this a moralist who seeks to lift the veil surrounding Mexican society's own feigned "innocence" in not clarifying or wishing to shed light on the motive behind José's suicide (somewhat akin to the speculation and invention of the tabloid press)? Is there a lesson to be found among the pages of the diary, a kind of encoded suicide note, that warns the reader of the consequences of obsessing on one's homoerotic desires? (Or is it a footnote to the story of one who refuses to call them by name?) Or is the lesson one for those who dwell on a single, romanticized object of desire when there are so many, many others available in the urban metropolis? (This would imply that José is an old-fashioned, far from open and modern, consumer whose future failure in this society is alluded to in Paredes Salas's "sermon" on homosexuality.) If the latter option is one way of filling in the spaces of the text, then the moral lesson would most certainly prefigure the character of Adonis García in Luis Zapata's 1979 novel, since Adonis very much takes this advice to heart in his "aventuras [y] desventuras" (adventures [and] misadventures) as the subtitle in Spanish suggests. Such a reading of Barbachano Ponce's novel connects the two narratives in a way not evident at first glance.

Notes

1   No reviews of the novel or articles dealing with its subject matter (or with its treatment of that subject matter) have been published in the United States. In Mexico, four brief review articles appeared the year of its publication in *Siempre!*, *El Universal*, and *El Nacional*. Of recent books on the novel in Mexico, only Foster's book mentions Barbachano Ponce at all.

2   See Schneider, 83. It is curious that in an otherwise carefully documented study of developments in the Mexican novel between 1968 and 1988 Steele cites the first gay male novel as Luis Zapata's *Las aventuras, desventuras y sueños de Adonis García, el vampiro de la colonia Roma* (1979) (*Adonis García*, 1981). Of the few novels that she includes in this category of analysis, she judges that "the best of these works to date is still the first one" (15), Zapata's text.

3   Mora notes that in 1958, the year Toledo is said to have lost his diary on a second-class bus, there were 375 films premiered in Mexico City, 183 of which were produced in the United States and 100 of which were Mexican. As for the movies of national origin, Mora summarizes: "The trend of Mexican cinema in the late 1950s was to make more 'spectacular' films in color, to utilize new techniques such as Cinemascope, and to inject a rather hesitant eroticism into standard melodramas by the display of nudity. This policy was designed, on the one hand, to draw domestic audiences away from television and, on the other, to make Mexican movies more competitive on the international scene. . . . Quality plummeted but production increased" (99). With the election of president Adolfo López Mateos, the film industry concentrated on making profits for a small group of investors and entrepreneurs, and on the representation on screen of a more conservative and disinterested vision of Mexican reality.

4   Formulaic films such as melodramas, the adventures of improbable superheroes, and teary sagas of distraught mothers sacrificing all to keep their families together still dominate the marketplace. The recordings and films of Libertad Lamarque, one of the only actresses mentioned by name in the text (61), are of particular interest to José. In moments of acute solitude he listens to her laments such as "Ya no me quieres" (You don't love me any more) and "Cuando vuelva a tu lado" (When I'm back by your side) and "reads" the lyrics as pertinent to his own sentiments. Such personal identification with popular music is played out across the majority of novels by Luis Zapata as well, even to the point of a character taking on the appearance and identity of the pop singer and actress Angélica María.

5   In a section of his book on the years 1942–58 and narrative developments during that time, Brushwood says of Fuentes's *La región más transparente* that it portrays a newly cosmopolitan Mexico City, one in which culture and commercial ventures thrive, and in which the opposition "hypocrisy versus authenticity" (53) is the marker of getting by and/or getting ahead. The sacrifice of one for the other, of reality for appearance (masquerade) is part and parcel of the internationalization of the Mexican economy and culture as well. But such a shift makes one suspect that collective or individual self-assurance might just as equally be another case of "hypocrisy" or spectacle put on in public for the benefit of a transnational audience (on the one hand) or, in the case of some, just plain survival. The Mexican government's official interest in externalizing an image of "modernity," which culminates in the Olympic Games hosted by Mexico in 1968 as a showcase for the nation's modernization, parallels the exhortation by Alberto Paredes Salas to José Toledo to play his role "straight" as one of the group of "nosotros los homosexuales." Rather than an organized collectivity, however, the "we" insinuated here seems more to go off in the direction of a hidden, underground, secret brotherhood based on some vague notion of affinity rather than suggesting concerted action or identity.

6   I use the term *testimony* in its broadest sense. In the literary and political schema presented by John Beverley, this diary-within-a-novel would most likely fall into the classification of a "pseudo*testimonio*" owing to its cult of individualism and its "inverting a form that grows out of subaltern experience into one that is middle-brow" (105). This is true, in particular, because of the novel's firm entrenchment in the urban middle class and in written culture. The same could be said for *Adonis García,* although it is presented as the written transcript of tape-recorded conversations. Yet the potential for each text to represent some aspects of the lives of Mexicans on the margins of "respectable" and "acceptable" culture is undeniably similar, if not equal, to the *testimonio*'s platform for the subaltern classes.

Works Cited

Abbott, Porter, Jr. *Diary Fiction: Writing as Action.* Ithaca, N.Y.: Cornell University Press, 1984.

Barbachano Ponce, Miguel. *El diario de José Toledo.* Mexico City: Private edition, published in Talleres de la Librería Madero, 1964. Copyright of the author.

Beverley, John. "The Margin at the Center: On *testimonio* (Testimonial Narrative)." In *De-Colonizing the Subject: The Politics of Gender in Women's Autobiography.* Ed. Sidonie Smith and Julia Watson. Minneapolis: University of Minnesota Press, 1992. 91–114.

Brushwood, John S. *Narrative Innovation and Political Change in Mexico.* New York: Peter Lang, 1989.

Foster, David William. *Gay and Lesbian Themes in Latin American Writing.* Austin: University of Texas Press, 1991.

Fuentes, Carlos. *La región más transparente.* 1958. Mexico City: Fondo de Cultura Económica, 1972.

———. *Where the Air is Clear: A Novel.* Trans. Sam Hileman. 1960. New York: Farrar, Straus and Giroux, 1985.

Garber, Marjorie. *Vested Interests: Cross-Dressing and Cultural Anxiety.* New York: Routledge, 1992.

Monsiváis, Carlos. "Notas sobre la cultura mexicana en el siglo XX." In *Historia general de México.* 3d ed., vol. 2. Mexico City: El Colegio de México, 1981. 1375–1548.

Mora, Carl J. *Mexican Cinema: Reflections of a Society 1896–1988.* Rev. ed. Berkeley: University of California Press, 1989.

Schneider, Luis Mario. "El tema homosexual en la nueva narrativa mexicana." *Casa del Tiempo* 5.49/50 (febrero/marzo 1985): 82–86.

Smith, Paul Julian. *Laws of Desire: Questions of Homosexuality in Spanish Writing and Film, 1960–1990.* Oxford: Oxford University Press, 1992.

Steele, Cynthia. *Politics, Gender, and the Mexican Novel, 1968–1988: Beyond the Pyramid.* Austin: University of Texas Press, 1992.

Zapata, Luis. *Adonis García: A Picaresque Novel.* Trans. Edward A. Lacey. San Francisco: Gay Sunshine Press, 1981.

———. *Las aventuras, desventuras y sueños de Adonis García, el vampiro de la colonia Roma.* Mexico City: Grijalbo, 1979.

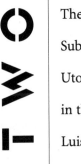

The Power of

Subversive Imagination:

Utopian Discourse

in the Novels of

Luis Zapata and

José Rafael Calva

El sexo polimorfo . . . : el fuego sagrado de Prometeo, la fuerza
que permitirá — acaso — la realización de la utopía.
[Polymorphous sex . . . : Prometheus's sacred fire, the force
which will allow — perhaps — the realization of utopia.]
— José Joaquín Blanco, "Ojos que da pánico soñar"

As Northrop Frye, Frank and Fritzie Manuel, and M. I. Finley, among others,
have demonstrated, the study of literary utopias calls forth a series of con-
comitant issues that must be addressed (though perhaps not resolved) by the
critic. This is particularly true for an examination of contemporary (postmodern) utopian visions, because they are at once the inheritors of a long tradition (what Finley refers to as an extensive "semantic cluster" [178]), as well as
varied and innovative responses to specific present-day societies.

Among these basic issues one must include an awareness and consideration
of the multiple definitions and plural aesthetic manifestations of utopias over
the centuries since the appearance in 1516 of Thomas More's now-classic text,
owing to the fact that utopian writing — like satire, the critical mode often
used in the construction of utopian texts — appears to adapt constantly in both
form and content to varying historical and social circumstances. (This occurs
as one set of needs is fulfilled and replaced by another in the endless search for

a better world which Tom Moylan calls the "utopian impulse" [20].) Among the wealth of allusions to the term *utopian* from the sixteenth century on, references have surfaced with both positive and pejorative connotations. These range, in brief, from "a merely derogatory epithet, connoting a wild fancy or a chimerical notion, . . . to an ideal psychological condition or to an idealizing capacity . . . [or even to] a dramatic narrative portrayal of a way of life that is so essentially good and fulfills so many profound longings that it wins immediate, almost instinctive, approbation" (Manuel and Manuel 2).

Whether it is used to refer to what are viewed as exotic and extravagant flights of private fantasy, to fundamentally ahistorical and impractical dreams of a golden age, or to actual generalized programs (or prescriptions) for future ideal societies, it is helpful as well as necessary to focus on the literary utopia using one prime consideration. That is, how does the producer of the work in question view the change from less than optimum *present* conditions to a *future* world of happiness and human satisfaction? This essay proposes to emphasize the not at all gratuitous relationship between present and future, following the critical opinions expressed by Finley and Moylan that utopian writing is rooted in specific classes, groups, and individuals in their unique historical contexts and therefore that "utopian ideas and fantasies, like all ideas and fantasies, grow out of the society to which they are a response" (Finley 180).

It is this very link with the present that contradicts the suggestion that utopias are by nature merely unattainable, impracticable, unrealizable fantasies. Utopian literature should be looked at instead as a kind of "crisis writing"; that is, its appearances throughout history coincide with and derive from moments of cultural crisis, transition, and dramatic change. This leads Frye to point out that it is this crucial "element of analysis, of criticism, . . . [that] brings important Utopias back from Nowhere to reality" (330, 339). Both Finley and the Manuels corroborate such an important alternative aspect of utopian thought in their commentaries on the origins of the word itself. Finley stresses what he calls an inherent pun in the term suggested in verses appended by More to his text: "The initial letter 'u' stands for the Greek ou ('no,' 'not') and hence Utopia is Nowhere. But by the exercise of a little imagination the 'u' can also stand for the Greek prefix eu ('good,' 'well') and then we get 'good place,' 'ideal place'" (Finley 178). A *locus amoenus,* an ideal place, concretizes the idea of utopian alternatives as opposed to the black hole of negative space ('nowhere'). 'Good places' are responses to dystopias (good places gone awry);

they resist the affirmations of dominant ideologies; they are spaces for the expression of oppressed desires and the assumption of human potential. They
comprise the realm of the imagination as well as that of actual geography. In
summary, they are examples of Ernst Bloch's "figures of hope" (Moylan 21)[1]
latent in the present and empowered by the forces of the imagination.

The deep social conflicts of the 1960s awakened a new form for the utopian impulse, an innovation that has played an important role in the con-
figuration and imagery of cultures — or subcultures — produced by a number
of groups opposed to contemporary society as structured by what can be defined as "the modern phallocratic capitalist system and the bureaucratic state"
(Moylan 15). (It must be pointed out, however, that there exist as well critical utopias voicing similar dissatisfaction with the promises of the Left.) These
postmodern "critical utopias" (the term is Moylan's) have as their premise to
echo yet at the same time to subvert accepted opinions of the day. In other
words, the vehicle of criticism is a so-called distorted model of one or more of
the precepts of mainstream culture, one of the master narratives whose very
mastery is placed in question (see Owens). The critical utopia concentrates in
particular on the values affirmed by a faceless and dehumanized technocratic
power structure, the effects of rampant consumer capitalism, and the conflicts
generated between affluent societies or social classes and the exploitation and
repression needed to maintain them. In short, subversive utopias are reactions
to capitalist dystopias; they offer examples of confrontations with capitalism's
failure to meet *real* human needs and desires (and of the substitution of the
false needs of the market in their place).

The composing of such literary texts is clearly a radical act in that they
dare to address utopian alternatives — albeit self-critically or parodically —
especially in a dystopian world. These projects are truly *critical* given that they
take on as adversaries both the historical situation and the utopian genre itself
in its twentieth-century use as the representation (justification) of either an
already-achieved perfection or an inevitable outcome of the current system if
left on its own. Each is revealed as myth in the subversion by utopia. (In her
examination of trends in North American fictional narrative, Nadia Khouri
views such an appropriation of utopias by the capitalist dream as "the bourgeois outlook that capitalism contain[s] the seeds of its own perfection" [105],
an obvious parody of Marx as well). Louis Marin discusses this utopic function
of discourses on utopia in terms of "a critique of dominant ideology insofar

as it is a reconstruction of contemporary society by means of a displacement and a projection of its structures into a fictional discourse. It is thus different from the philosophical discourse of ideology, which is the totalizing expression of reality as it is given, and of its ideal justification. Utopia displaces and projects this reality in the form of a nonconceptional fictional totality. Reality [therefore] takes the form of a figure produced in and by discourse" (Marin 195). Such a "reconstruction" allows for the fragmentation of the "totalizing" concept underpinning ideologies and for the emptying of the so-called absolute realm of the real of any of its former "natural" or naturalized values.

Turning our attention to a specific case, two superb examples of postmodern critical utopias are to be found among recent works of Mexican fiction in Luis Zapata's *Las aventuras, desventuras y sueños de Adonis García, el vampiro de la colonia Roma (Adonis García: A Picaresque Novel)* and José Rafael Calva's *Utopía gay* (Gay utopia). Of the Latin American countries, Mexico is perhaps among those most obviously caught in the cross fire of international capitalism's effects, at least in part because of its geographic position as either buffer or battle zone between the United States and the rest of mainland Latin America. Both texts were written during the *sexenio* or six-year presidential term of López Portillo (1976–82) — although it took Calva six years to finally get his published — a period more than ten years after the protests and massacres of 1968, and during the peak of Mexican oil boom prosperity. These are the years before the political scandals involving Police Chief Durazo and the economic crises (dystopias) of the oil price bust of the 1980s. During this period, in general terms, economic benefits from the oil industry intensified class contradictions — such as the definition of just who would be the recipients of these profits and how they were to be disbursed — and the government continued trying to fill the cultural "void" left after the end of the 1960s. The serious questioning of social values during previous decades could no longer be dismissed out of hand; Mexico was beginning to take the first steps on a road to prosperity unexpected before the discovery of the vast oil reserves and had to create an image of democracy if the international market was to respond to its offers. The newly resuscitated class warfare, effecting a closing of the ranks to jealously keep a lid on the distribution of economic benefits, was complemented by an increase in consumer spending on the part of the middle classes promoted by the government as compensation for a lack of real participation in the national political affairs of a patriarchal state.[2] The 1970s and early 1980s reflected what was, in essence, the entrenchment of capitalist fantasies of production and consumption in Mexican society under a system that functioned primarily by means of "reification and exploitation—that transformation of human relations and unrestricted nature into the appearance of relationships between things that can be produced and consumed, bought and sold" (Moylan 16). (In the 1990s, Mexican journalist Guadalupe Loaeza refers to the most recent outcome of this acquisition-based social identity, beyond the limits of basic human necessity, in a twist on Descartes's philosophical theory "Cogito, ergo sum" (I think, therefore I am). She rewrites it as "Compro, luego existo" (I buy, therefore I am) and uses this concept as her premise for studying the manic buying frenzy of Mexican consumers.)

It is modern Mexico's dehumanization, banalization, and commercialization of human relationships around which both Zapata's and Calva's texts revolve. These are the very myths (or ideological webs) placed in fragmentary form into the "reconstructed fictions" (after Marin) of their narratives. Both works represent first-person voices belonging to one of the most important but traditionally marginalized minority groups in that society, homosexuals, whose discourse intimately and permanently links utopia to dystopia in an attempt to break "la unanimidad imprescindible para establecer una dominación vertical en la sociedad" (the unanimity indispensable in order to establish vertical domination [authority] in society) (Blanco 184). This vertical hierarchy—which sanctions appropriate and *productive* behavior that is morally, economically, and politically in line with the officially recognized values of marriage, child-bearing, etc.—demands dependence; social, political, and sexual repression; the valorization of possessions and property (human or otherwise); and (last but not least) "la renuncia pública al placer" (the public renunciation of pleasure) (Monsiváis 20). The sublimation of desire —whatever form of fantasy it might take—is also understood allegorically as the reflection of a more general social repression of what Marcuse calls "the pleasure principle," modern capitalism's sacrifice to the "reality principle" of productivity.[3] Resistance is tamed through such sublimation.

Gay utopian narrative is one more "space" that is in the process of being created in Mexican literature and culture. What has been called the "gay theme or motif" (Salazar 10)[4] began to make its appearance furtively in the pages of Mexican prose writing long before Zapata and Calva. At the beginning of the decade of the sixties, homosexual characters were already wandering through the novels and stories of writers such as Carlos Fuentes (in *Cambio de piel* [*A Change of Skin*]), Luisa Josefina Hernández (*Nostalgia de Troya* [Nostalgia for Troy]), Sergio Fernández (*Los peces* [The fish], *Segundo sueño* [*A Second Dream*]), and even Juan José Arreola (*La feria* [*The Fair*]), just to mention a few examples. In these instances, however, the so-called "gay motif" is barely developed, often quite tangentially, as something circumstantial to the central plot or contingent upon it to the extent that there is no exploration or interest beyond the superficial — or sympathy-provoking — presentation of a character. With *Adonis García* and *Utopía gay* the reader becomes aware of a commitment to a different worldview that conditions the entire narrative. The politics of these texts are contingent upon themselves and their agendas, not on any general thematics. The "theme" has become a political issue of representation and self-representation through the literary text and its formal devices.

By choosing to defend oppositional modes of both sexual and textual expression that might be censured by society as extraordinary (outside the "ordinary," whatever that might imply) under its codes of social and material (re)production, these writers and their narrators are opting at the same time for what they imagine as a *political difference* in all aspects of life. Theirs is an open act of negating the power of the present by imagining instead "la realidad del sexo sin subterfugios" (the reality of sex without subterfuges [pretexts]) (Blanco 1981 189), "autonomy, mutual aid, and equality," "reciprocity, tenderness, spontaneity" (Moylan, 27, 12), and a whole range of activities and fantasies unrelated to profits and commodities but oriented rather toward "giving, creating, and aesthetic enjoyment . . . , the realization of physical, sensuous, and intellectual capacities" (Gorz 81). All this without slighting any one aspect for the others. This is reflected, for instance, in the affirmations of the epigraphs from Walt Whitman's *Song of Myself* and Carlos Pellicer's poetry in *Utopía gay*. Adonis García, the "vampire" of Zapata's text, is not just "un acostón bien pagado" (a well-paid lay) as the book jacket of Zapata's later novel *En jirones* claims; he *is* that, but he is more. He sings of the joys of his activities even while he finds some of the drawbacks to them; yet they are never enough to keep him off the streets for very long. Adonis, like *Utopía gay*'s Adrián and Carlos, is an individual who insists on "el sexo y . . . el cuerpo como formas radicales de vida, fuentes de transformación y creatividad, que irradian su energía a todos los actos cotidianos" (sex and the body as radical forms of life, sources of transformation and creativity, that irradiate their energy to all daily activities) (Blanco 1981, 184). The transformative aspect of everyday life is a utopian vision, one of Moylan's utopian impulses, if ever there were one. One need look no farther than surrounding circumstances for the space of change, and both Zapata and Calva envision transformations in the social relations they see around them by offering their characters a choice (at the end of each text). Rather than selecting between this world and another—even if Adonis does fantasize a spaceship to transport him to a new supply of lovers elsewhere in the solar system the choice actually involves the continuation of the utopian impulse or its abandonment.[5]

In order to encounter the roots of these dystopian targets, the novels reflect the urban present in which the characters live. Their venue is the Distrito Federal, Mexico's capital city, as the prime center for the experience of human alienation. Clearly, situating fictional narratives in this metropolis is not of itself innovative. It does exemplify, however, one of several directions of post-boom narrative in Mexico (and, I hazard the generalization, in Latin America) in its "decentered" portrait of gay resistance and newfound hope among those in these anonymous urban magnets of capitalist dreams. As the critic García Aguilar very concisely sums up the literary panorama of the last ten to fifteen years, "Los nuevos autores han escogido varios caminos: unos tomaron el de la recreación histórica, volviendo a hablar de héroes legendarios de batallas lejanas y recientes, otros han dado fuerza a la recreación de sagas provincianas, y los demás ofrecen el testimonio de la desesperanza urbana" (The new authors have chosen various paths: some have taken the path of historical recreation, once again talking about legendary heroes of battles both long ago and recent, others have reinforced the re-creation of provincial sagas, and the rest offer testimony to urban desperation) (14). In this dystopian urban setting the critical utopian vision reacts with sarcasm to the official version of a present earthly paradise represented by the marketplace—department stores such as El Palacio de Hierro, and shopping malls modeled after Perisur are the cornerstones of this world—as the new Garden of Eden. Through several of their characters, Zapata and Calva satirize, via an incessant "consumption" of bodies, the modern reverence for the accumulation of property and the fetishizing of money in order to "belong" to the so-called miracle of Mexican progress and modernity. *Utopía gay* takes one step beyond in its satire of the fertile, productive womb and, simultaneously, society's vision of the "unproductive," infertile homosexual couple as well as socioeconomic dictatorship over desire. The text does so by means of staging Adrián's pregnancy, the point of departure and central theme around which this Joycean-style narrative is woven, from the first pages containing Adrián's internal monologue on the possible origins and consequences of his situation, through the last, which contain his dreams for the future. Both monologues and dialogues in the text form counterpoints of contrasting views about a vast array of topics such as androgyny and bisexuality, political commitment, the persecution of homosexuals, social and economic frustration, the rising incidence of gay suicide in the D.F., and individual desires that personalize history against a suggested background of more objective events and issues. This panorama includes political corruption, medical care, petroleum production, union activism in the UNAM (National Autonomous University of Mexico), the influx of United States cultural artifacts including Alice Cooper recordings and Levi's jeans, and the daily challenges of surviving as a gay man in what Adrián calls a "fascist" society (34). This particular aspect of Calva's work personifies what Marin considers the critical function of utopic dialogue — here, monologue — as "picture and representation," the conjuring up of "a negative referent" (79) against which flexible and malleable utopian space may be opened up.

Zapata's updated, twentieth-century version of the traditional first-person picaresque narrative is a seven-cassette "testimonial" by Adonis García, alias the vampire, to his psychiatrist. These recorded narratives constantly pit the individual desires of the "I" against what is socially "acceptable" (as represented by the psychiatrist's commentary to which Adonis responds but which is a silence on the tapes, an absence except as a subtext running behind or beside the audible words of the patient). The complete title of the novel in Spanish gives the reader a hint as to this contrapuntal narrative, aside from echoing the tradition of the picaresque text's series of episodes. The joining together of the "adventures, misadventures (misfortunes), and dreams" of Adonis García exemplifies Moylan's utopian impulse, the search for a better world within the concrete conditions surrounding this character. This is a social situation that he realizes will continue to leave him out if relationships here and now are an indication of the future. His recurring dreams — of narrow stairways, speeding motorcycles, claustrophobic trains, and swimming against the current of a raging river — are ever-present signs of the resistance he faces every day. Yet he never ceases to swim, ride, walk, or keep on moving in spite of the hindrances he finds in his path. The voyage motif is a vestige of the picaresque, certainly, but in Zapata's text it is also a reaffirmation of the will of the character to survive and not be engulfed and swept away into an undifferentiated social stream.

In an obvious parody of the capitalist system's work ethic, with its emphasis on production, accumulation, regulated leisure, and conspicuous consumption, the more he works the streets the less Adonis accumulates in his coffers and the less satisfied he is. He becomes deeply depressed at the thought of charging for sex as a business obligation instead of an act of pleasure, but quickly gets caught up in "la fiebre del oro" (gold fever) (213) once he is exposed to the variety and possibilities of the market. Adonis's immediate dreams take the form of having a private telephone installed in his room and eating in expensive restaurants, because as a consumer he believes he deserves the right to enjoy more luxuries, just as the mass media tells him he ought to. The temptations don't seem to convince him, though, and he finds the economic substitute for physical pleasure a poor one. In the end he reaches the conclusion that it is submission to this created system of (false) economic needs and rewards that has been the greatest impediment to his happiness and the direct cause of his alcoholism. Adonis tells his listener that "como que siempre el . . . estar jodido económicamente te chinga otros aspectos de tu vida te chinga en tus relaciones con los demás" (it's like . . . always being economically screwed up messes up other aspects of your life it screws you up in your relations with everyone else) (90). He has witnessed this process of economic demand not only in his own life but in the breakup of his family, the suffering of relatives, and with the few friends he has made in the city as a result of working the bars, cafés, tourist areas, and streets. (The friends are few because of petty rivalries, jealousies, and competition for clients among those who inhabit the streets.) Through "el vampiro," whose epithet evokes the image of a subhuman nocturnal life-stealing creature parasitically living off others, the reader perceives both the young man's vivid dreams of pleasure and the inflationary spiral in the Mexican economy as the society pleasurably consumes more goods, as reflected in the rising prices of the "taloneadores" (streetwalkers) in the "gran fraternidad" (great brotherhood) (61) of the utopian space of the Zona Rosa (tourist Pink Zone) and the colonia Roma. The latter, a residential district in the heart of downtown Mexico City, was a space that epitomized "progressive" thinking between the decades of the sixties and the early seventies. It has since become only a pale reminder of those spirited times as economic decay and the 1985 earthquake have eaten away at urban areas and as the new wealthy move to the suburbs or to the more rural spaces left in the state of Mexico outside the capital. Even in 1979, the promises held out by the colonia Roma reflect a greater proportion of nostalgia than reality.

In *Utopía gay,* Carlos and Adrián have seen and lived firsthand the depoliticizing of Mexico after 1968, the years when protest and opposition were absorbed by the established political hierarchy through the appropriation and sanitization of fashion, music, and other subcultural expressions of protest into commercial objects of mass production and equally fervent mass consumption. Stylish blue jeans replace the workers' overalls, muzak takes the bite out of rock, and the concept of "lifestyle" intrudes on the issue of class. Carlos's observation of those around him as living "en una orgía perpetua con la materia" (in a perpetual orgy with material goods) (19) leads him to exalt the erotic as a compensatory utopia of self-realization. Having been a politically committed philosophy professor and former student leader in the sixties and early seventies, Carlos now finds that in the process he has been sublimating his own needs and desires. He reaches the decision that "lo cierto es que mi homosexualidad es más importante que tener al dedillo el desenvolvimiento de la política internacional porque lo mío lo vivo de cerca" (the truth is that my homosexuality is more important than having at my fingertips the unfolding of international politics because my life is what I live up close [firsthand]) (170). In a confessional-type examination of the past, Carlos now turns away from one type of political radicalism toward another: his commitment to Adrián, their unborn child, and a new life of political opposition and difference. He calls this decision "la encarnación de mi voluntad y mis sentimientos" (the incarnation of my will and [deepest] beliefs or sentiments) (67). The exact form of this utopia is left open, however, because the event that will precipitate it—the birth of Carlos Adrián—has yet to occur, even at the end of the novel.

In order to break down the pretended coherence of the "leyenda negra" (black legend) (49) that Mexican society has imposed on the subject of homosexuality and the gay community, Calva uses humor and the potential for word play in colloquial language to express the very human wants of his characters. In fact, the very "blackness" of the image of homosexuality is changed by the everyday preoccupations of Carlos and Adrián, their parody of heterosexuality; the end result is the demythification of the "leyenda" as such as an ideological creation. Calva attacks the norms of biological and cultural control by making the centerpiece of the narrative the "antiaesthetic" bulge of Adrián's pregnancy. Being the first "padrimadre" (fathermother) (174) in history and therefore a scientific—and social—novelty that the characters feel doctors would want to exploit commercially, Adrián is the focus of two crucial concepts. The first is the desire to contradict the "no-reproducción obligatoria" (obligatory nonreproduction) (74) of the traditionally dictated social and physical roles of these two men to represent instead the imagined fulfillment of his dream of having a child with his lover Carlos. For Adrián, the child's conception, whether actually effected or a projection of his own wishful thinking, represents a challenge in defiance of those who would scoff at such a desire. The second aspect is the utopian world, which the existence of this child—or the hope for the existence of this child—stimulates as a "figure of hope" to be opened up for them by his or her arrival. (I say his or her, but they take for granted that the child will be male.) Although they admit that their offspring will encounter "más hostilidad que si fuera el anticristo" (more hostility than if it were the Antichrist) (13), at they same time they see the child as an impetus toward their salvation.

The special significance of the child's conception positions this offspring as the catalyst for some sort of an apocalyptic moment at which the utopian impulse would cease to be an intangible wish and would take on concrete form. "Un hijo que nos pudiera sacar de este mundo" (a child who could take us out of this world) (171), says Carlos, is his fantasy, since they propose to be the Adam and Eve (plus one) of a new social order on their own in Baja California. At this point the utopian impulse would distance itself (and them) from the urban surroundings to which they have reacted, and it would carry them elsewhere to begin again. In this peculiar manner, then, the urban dystopia leads to a utopian vision contrary to that of Ariel Dorfman's character in *The Last Song of Manuel Sendero*. In that novel, a fetus refuses to be born until circumstances outside the womb improve. In *Utopía gay,* the child itself will be the beginning of an alteration in social circumstances. Desired or real, Carlos and Adrián's child is the agent that catalyzes their utopian visions.

Zapata's and Calva's texts propose utopias on various levels as alternatives to the preceding conditions, which their characters witness as obstacles to the plenitude of human pleasure and satisfaction. Their recovery and centering of human desire from its ghettoization as reprobate or restricted activity (when, where, how, with whom) liberates spaces for the gratification of this desire rather than its continued frustration. These images (mental representations) and figures (bodily forms) assume diverse shapes that can be classified as utopias of physical liberation, psychological liberation, and textual liberation.

Physical liberation here suggests intimacy as a political act of unpostponed desire that need not be covered up with the semblance of "acceptable" behavior or relegated to a shadowy world of official nonexistence. Glimpses of what at the time seem to be liberated spaces appear repeatedly in the everyday lives of Adonis, Carlos, and Adrián. Yet they are often merely shifts in direction or changes in geography in the hope of *finding* an improved situation. (The quote from Francisco de Quevedo's picaresque text *La historia de la vida del Buscón* [The story of the life of the Buscón], used as an epigraph for the last section of Zapata's novel, reflects this hope that changing location will better his life. It is a staple of the myths included in the picaresque genre.) These ingenuous "brushes with utopia" take the shape of flights from sexual repression: from the provinces (Guanajuato) to the capital; from one *colonia* or district of the city to another in search of adventure; from one body to the next seeking the short-term utopia of "the new," as when Adonis tells of his longing to continually "probar nuevos chavos" (try out [sample] new boys) (98). They also include the artificial euphoria of drugs and alcohol used to forget reality and "feel good";[6] the secret underworld of public baths—what Calva's characters refer to as a "submundo" (subcultural world) (77)—which create the illusion of an atmosphere of equality wherein all naked bodies are classless and interested only in collective cooperation to satisfy the desires of any and all present; and movie theaters, both to escape into the perfect images projected on the screen and to look for lovers among those in the audience. Adonis García even makes the observation that in these environments "se pierden todos los egoísmos" (all selfishness and egotism disappears) (Zapata 201), thereby stressing the socially alternative nature of the space.

These experiences do appropriate the oppositional "culture of the night"—streets, public restrooms, Sanborn's restaurants, nightclubs, urban mansions—as a zone somehow liberated from the dominant ideologies at work during the day. Perhaps these seem to be just another set of illusions, but they are also the euphoric experiences of the late seventies when Mexican gay liberation groups began to flourish and when young men like Adonis flocked to the city filled with dreams of expending unrestricted libidinal energy. Instead of society's enclosing or entrapping their hunger for pleasure, these characters are inserted into a (fictional) night world with open frontiers. This is a fact echoed in the words of Adonis—"el vampiro"—himself when he confesses in a moment of epiphany that "me di cuenta de que la vida vale únicamente por los placeres que te puede dar que todo lo demás son pendejadas y que si uno no es feliz es por pendejo" (I realized that life's value comes only from the pleasures it can give you that all the rest is foolishness and if someone isn't happy it's because he's a jerk) (53). The streets are his cafeteria of options, and Adonis generously samples from all those available. Even the image of the vampire, a characterization frequently directed against gay men and lesbians,[7] becomes rehumanized in Zapata's novel: Adonis is not presented as a specter wandering during the predawn hours feeding off the blood of so-called innocents. In fact, he is frequently the real victim of abuse by others. Rather than economic remuneration (the maximum yield for the minimum effort), his real hunger is not for devouring flesh but for experiencing reciprocal pleasure and acceptance. These are also the principal elements cementing the relationship between Adrián and Carlos, who are as uninhibited in describing their physical desires to the reader as they are in satisfying those desires with each other. The revelation, exploration, and elaboration of these individual utopian dreams—in vivid contrast but in close proximity to repressive reality—forms the basis of both texts.

Psychological liberation, on the other hand, is the power to imagine a "gay utopia" in as many variations as there are participants in its formation. Adonis García commences the process of constructing the image of a reality or space in which he might feel free while lying on the psychiatrist's couch. There he begins to realize that there is a big difference between what Calva's characters refer to as "*la* realidad" and "*nuestra* realidad" (reality/our reality) (60; my emphasis). This corresponds to what José Joaquín Blanco writes of as "la necesidad de inventarse una vida" (the need to invent [imagine] a life for yourself) (183) in a traditional society such as Mexico. This invention starts with the visions of critical utopias and figures of hope found in the two fictional narratives under consideration. And the goal of such imaginings is not the recovered innocence of a lost paradise that has been consumed by the present dystopia but instead a consciousness of needing to *build* alternatives, ones perhaps radically different from anything that has existed before. Both Adrián and Adonis come to the realization that none of what they want will happen magically without their committed participation. At the very minimum, the imagination involved in these discourses presents possible solutions to the contradictions between reality and desire, between "reality" and "our reality." Within the boundaries of the city or elsewhere, Adonis, Carlos, and Adrián have to consider their choices for "inventing" a life if they want it to be any different from what they have experienced so far.

Both novels are at least able to create images of future scenarios of egalitarian, non-exploitative utopian societies.[8] Each envisions a "day of liberation" that actually signifies a day of self-liberation. At the end of Zapata's novel, Adonis García takes the first step in the conception of this freedom by telling his analyst that when he tires of the sameness of people and places in Mexico City, he pictures a group of Martians making contact with him. He also imagines them being acquainted with his sexual powers, as word has spread throughout the known universe, giving him unprecedented extraterrestrial fame. He then departs with them, willingly leaving behind the earth and all of its oppressions. Adonis describes imagining himself inside a spaceship rushing away from the Angel of Independence, the Monument to the Revolution, Mexico, the American continent, and finally earth itself. At this point he closes his eyes and makes a wish never to return to the life he has left behind. Nevertheless, the narrative stops short at this moment without giving more details of this utopian dream, allowing for an infinity of imagined versions and interpretations. While many of them might include a happier version of Adonis, at least one must consider the implications of his confessions to the psychiatrist and the role of this figure in the channeling of "aberrant" dreams and fictions into more socially "appropriate" and productive forms. Will the therapy sessions and drugs make Adonis accept the limitations on his happiness and adapt to them, will they redirect his longings in other ways, or will they quash his utopian dreams?

In *Utopía gay* the reader finds a continuation of almost the same thought in Adrián's wish to return to human nature by means of a return to nature itself. To find harmony and to "ransom" life from "la computadora y la xeromanía . . . [y] la tevé [con] su cotidiana labor de envilecimiento del hombre" (computers and Xerox-mania . . . [and] TV [with] its daily task of degrading mankind) (Calva Pratt 52), he envisions the ultimate dystopia of an atomic war that kills two-thirds of humanity in order to create the necessary requirements of space for cultivating both land and love in an idyllic utopian setting. This is a real vision of apocalyptic cleansing. When he declares that "sólo en el estado salvaje la armonía es real" (only in the savage [natural] state is there real harmony) (84), Adrián is summarizing his paean to the unrepressed body—his, Carlos's, and that of their child, who they hope will live a truly liberated life after they pave the way for him. The problem is that the obliteration of any trace of today's society seems to be the prerequisite.

Each of these characters represents an individual attempt at salvation, not an effort to mobilize communities or masses. Rather, as in the definitions presented at the beginning of this essay, there is an "idealizing capacity," the conceptualizing of a "good place," that marks both texts. It appears as if this personalization is a logical conclusion to events, since organized opposition to social and economic policies, now a thing of the past, has been eroded slowly during the last twenty years of Mexican history. If many intellectuals such as Carlos have become part of the government's homogenizing dream to create "change from within," the lower classes have had to reconsider their options as well. On the other hand, Adrián and Carlos review their alternatives and conclude that they must create a space for themselves and their new social order on the Sea of Cortés now that they have discovered this potential for happiness. Carlos ponders the situation at some length:

> . . . largarse y abandonar a la sociedad ya no es un crimen de evasión porque cuando una sociedad está mal pero tiene remedio y puede canalizarse la insatisfacción politizando al pueblo . . . oquey . . . pero cuando ya no se trata de una evasión sino el abandono de la sociedad gangrenada cancerosa y a punto de morir sin remedio posible es más inteligente pensar en irse . . . para en un lugar apartado pensar en la nueva cultura en la que pueda partirse de un concepto humano igualitario y democrático. (182–183)
> [. . . to run off and abandon society isn't a crime of evasion any more because when a society is in bad shape but there is still hope (for a solution) and dissatisfaction can be channeled by politicizing the population . . . OK . . . but when you're no longer talking about escaping from but rather about abandoning a gangrenous, cancer-ridden society on the verge of death without any possible cure it is smarter to think of getting away . . . so that in a remote place you can think about the new culture whose point of departure can be a democratic concept of human equality.]

Such a utopia responds to reality by transforming its bases—not forgetting its existence, since any utopian alternative is actually a response *to it*—into a new and, it is hoped, better human construct than before. And yet this is not the end of the process either. The construct, by definition, must change unceasingly in reaction to additional "democratic" impulses represented by relations among social, political, economic, and sexual equals. In other words, there is no final point but permanent impulse. Only the point of departure—human equality and democracy—is clearly set out.

The third facet of utopia is a liberation of the fictional text from the mediation of an authoritative voice (its own master narrative). In the case of Zapata's novel this allows Adonis García's words and perceptions to go, one assumes, straight from the tape recorder to the reader/listener without the interference or censorship of either grammatical correction or moral comment. At least this is the illusion tacitly proposed in the text. Given the work as fiction, however, one must keep in mind the existence of authorial criteria at some level, even if this normally suppressed voice of an unrecognized life is finally allowed to speak with a certain measure of freedom. This accent on immediacy is also true of *Utopía gay*'s alternating internal monologue/dialogue structure, in which both Carlos's and Adrián's most intimate thoughts are made accessible directly to the consumer of the text. In order to distance himself even more, Calva includes a "prologue" three-quarters of the way through the book in an effort to minimize any connection between implied author and narrators. It produces a simultaneous commentary on the order of traditional literary structures. But these are not authors who abandon their characters to possible condemnation by a restrictive reading while saving themselves from any responsibility for their stories. The distancing mechanism is merely a literary device. What Calva's short intercalated section does, though, is establish the text itself as a locus for the utopia of the writer. In a reconnection of inner and outer worlds, the text recovers the space of private dreams and fantasies that the author imagines and gives aesthetic substance by means of this novel. He writes that he fears the intimate nature of the pregnant man theme could be connected too personally to his own lover's desires (see 157), but that the actual image of his vision of utopia is the surrounding text, a situation that results in a very personal challenge. The author writes: "Precisamente eso en mi texto hizo que mi propia utopía se volviera un reto para mí extraliterariamente y fuera de la novela, porque la homosexualidad hoy está muy injustamente reprimida al punto que por ejemplo en México oficialmente no existe"

(It is precisely this in my text which made my own utopia become a challenge for me extraliterarily and outside the novel, because homosexuality today is very unjustly repressed to the point that in Mexico, for example, it does not officially exist at all) (159). That is to say, how does one link the freedom of the imagination on the page with the world in which one lives? Is there some correspondence between Carlos and Adrián's decision to flee the "cancerous society" for a better place, and the novelist who seeks to write him- or herself into existence through a world of words when the world of everyday acts denies any implementation of whatever dreams he or she might have? Is the literary text converted into the only space for utopia?

One of the principal aims of both *Adonis García* and *Utopía gay* is to bring out into the open agora of discourse a "nonconsumer" version of gay life in Mexican society of the time. This is a very difficult task, in particular since the renewed repression of liberation movements that began in 1978 when international gay communities publicly demonstrated their organizing power for the first time. The reaction to gay pride marches in Mexico was twofold. First was the temptation to revert to more insidious methods of control under the guise of protecting society from internal threats and dangers, which now appeared more numerous than some would ever have admitted. *And* they were organized. Second was an effort to turn the political implications of these communities into a source of economic consumption. As long as there is no "threat" of any real influence on the values and structures of society, there can exist the truce of a "tolerancia sexual del consumo" (sexual tolerance by consumer society) (Blanco 184). Because both novels were published after 1978, they fall into the territory of this debate. The forces in contention make up a false sexual democracy that allows for the "tolerated" space of gay bars, nightclubs, cabarets, etc., where entrepreneurs can take advantage of a new economic force in the country, which must be dealt with before it can turn its power to other (personal and/or political) uses. The creation of a sense of alterity, of a presence within the society but not blindly accepting of it without question, is another story. Adrián's mother is a good example of the middle classes' professed open mind toward homosexuality. She is reticent but willing to entertain her son and his lover in her home, up until the point when Adrián announces he is expecting a child. She refuses to believe it, then disowns him, then asks him why he isn't at least the "active" member of the couple. In the end, she concludes it is all a joke to embarrass her. The tolerance only goes so far. And it applies only to those who remain relatively invisible to the scrutiny of the public eye.

Carlos summarizes the situation when he laments the masquerade of tolerance by a society that is capable of absorbing difference and of marketing a harmless version of any alternative political, social, or sexual identity. He says, "lo que es imposible es escandalizar porque hasta de nosotros los *gays* se habla así como de menonitas o maoístas pues ya en cartelera se ve siempre anunciada una obra *gay* o un *show* de trasvestistas . . . y quienes llenan los teatros son familias porque a nosotros . . . ya nos aburren esas cosas en que se ve lo mismo que en nuestras fiestas de hace cincuenta años . . . y sabemos que lo mismo da que los bugas lo concienticen o no pues seguirán pensando lo mismo de nosotros pero ahora poniéndose en la pose *open mind* de dientes para afuera" (what is impossible nowadays is to cause a scandal because you can even talk about us gays, just like you talk about Mennonites or Maoists, since today you can see announcements on billboards for a gay show or a transvestite revue . . . and theaters are filled with families because we . . . are already bored with those scenes where you see the same things that you saw in our parties fifty years ago . . . and we know that it makes no difference whether straight people become aware of it or not since they will keep on thinking of us in the same way while they now affect the pose of open-mindedness, [at least] on the surface) (170). The stage show breaks down in the streets where Adonis and his friends try to survive once the mask of tolerance is removed.

Daring to propose these human voices of liberation and difference, as opposed to the stereotyped images of "locas" (queens) accepted by liberal proponents of "commiseration" (Blanco 188), is the last potential utopian alternative offered by these narratives to the dilemma of socioeconomic servitude from which their visions stem. Both narratives focus on valuing the political economy of the body's desires and longings as the point of departure for shaping possible future utopias. But they still must live in the present. Neither work proposes a static blueprint for happiness but rather a declaration of permanent opposition as "what is not yet is imagined by those seeking to engage what is" (Moylan 209).

Notes

1   A more thorough explanation of this concept is found in Bloch's *Principle of Hope.*

2   Richard Tardanico sees this authoritarian state and the simultaneous opening of the door to capitalism as long-range results of the interests that triumphed in the Mexican Revolution earlier in the twentieth century (see 757–758).

3   See Marcuse's *Eros and Civilization* for a thorough discussion of this concept. In addition, it is important to note that Calva's character Carlos seems to agree with the critic Monsiváis on the extension of the idea of the reification of human relationships to cover the economic production systems of *both* the "First" and "Second" Worlds. (Though the Soviet Union as the personification of the "Second World" has ceased to exist in the 1990s, it was certainly still a factor to be dealt with at the time of publication of these novels.) Monsiváis writes: "En lo general, la izquierda ha duplicado la ortodoxia conservadora: una política sexual partidaria de la familia como núcleo intocable, defensa de la monogamia estricta para la mujer, rechazo (por estrategia antimperialista) del control de la natalidad" (In general, the Left has duplicated the same conservative orthodoxy: a politics of sexuality that advocates the family as an untouchable nucleus, the strict defense of monogamy for the woman, the rejection [as anti-imperialist strategy] of birth control) (33). In the case of Latin America, it is clear that Cuba has long been considered by many as a prime example of this triumph of traditional ideology linked to socialist goals as far as the political/sexual body is concerned. Adrián mocks the abdication of responsibility over one's own body, whether responding to a politics of the Right or of the Left, on the very first page of *Utopía gay:* "si ni remotamente me había cuidado porque jamás pensé que pudiera quedar encinta . . . [la gente típicamente] vive sin cuidarse y delega a ellos [las bodegas, los consultorios] la responsabilidad de cuidar su cuerpo" (It didn't even remotely occur to me to take precautions because I never thought I could get pregnant . . . [people typically] live without being careful and they delegate to others [pharmacies, clinics] the responsibility of taking care of their bodies) (11).

4   The term is used by Salazar, whose 1987 article offers a concise review and overview of the recent history of gay literature in Mexico.

5   I am grateful to one of the Press's readers of this manuscript for pointing out the connection between Adonis García's real or imagined journeys and the travels to America of picaresque characters such as the Buscón and Moll Flanders. Such shared visions of "elsewhere" — maybe no place, maybe a real place — as the space for personal happiness seem to help position Zapata's texts within a literary tradition that has flourished in Spain and Latin America. It is curious to note that, for the European narrator, the New World is the site for such a quest (even for Camilo

José Cela's character Pascual Duarte, who, on the eve of the Spanish Civil War, yearns to escape his "criminal fate" by embarking on a journey from Galicia to America), while for Adonis García the hope of the metropolis has been exhausted. A new option opens up on a very twentieth-century frontier. By 1979, space is no longer "where no man has gone before," but it still offers the chance to imagine a new beginning. All of the characters mentioned live on society's margins in one sense or another, and all envision finding a "better place" already established, one to which they merely have to transport themselves in order to find utopian conditions. Adonis goes so far as to hope that his reputation as a lover will precede him to outer space, where he will be welcomed with open arms, no questions asked.

6   Adonis claims that alcohol "es para animarse" (is to cheer you up) (137). Carlos adds that "el alcohol . . . te sostiene y euforiza" (alcohol picks you up and makes you feel euphoric) (79). Both comments reflect its use in the quest for a sense of corporal well-being and joy.

7   Andrea Weiss's recent book entitled *Vampires and Violets: Lesbians in Film* addresses the horror film genre and its representation of lesbian vampires in films and other texts from the United States, Europe, and Latin America. The vampire metaphor, fluctuating between the reader's or observer's desire and fear, is explored in tales such as that of Transylvanian countess Elizabeth Bathory, the Bloody Countess, and her representation in a variety of visual and written texts including that of writer Alejandra Pizarnik. See also Bonnie Burns's recent article on the film *Dracula's Daughter,* in which lesbians are studied both as the images of the cinematic text *and* as the flickering light — now visible, now extinguished — of the apparatus (camera, film, lens, projector, screen) itself (197). Suzanne Chávez Silverman examines the intimate links between lesbian writing and invisibility in Pizarnik's *La condesa sangrienta* (The bloody countess) and the "conspiracy" of silence surrounding both the author and her work. Chávez Silverman's argument explores in this example of Spanish-American literature some of the categories used by Terry Castle in her subtle and suggestive analysis of the lesbian-vampire connection in British and American film and literature. Castle's proposal to study the lesbian-vampire motif in terms of the socially undead and invisible — hidden from history, overlooked, made transparent, casting no shadow, etc. — is a groundbreaking discussion in this area.

8   These characteristics are important, since, as Finley underscores in his discussion, there exist both hierarchical and egalitarian literary utopias.

Works Cited

Arreola, Juan José. *The Fair.* Trans. John Upton. Austin: University of Texas Press, 1977.
———. *La feria.* Mexico City: Joaquín Mortiz, 1963.
Blanco, José Joaquín. "Eyes I Dare Not Meet in Dreams." Trans. Edward A. Lacey. In *Gay Roots: Twenty Years of Gay Sunshine.* Ed. Winston Leyland. San Francisco: Gay Sunshine Press, 1991. 291–296.
———. "Ojos que da pánico soñar." In *Función de medianoche: Ensayos de literatura cotidiana.* 1979. Mexico City: Era, 1981. 181 190.
Bloch, Ernst. *The Principle of Hope.* Trans. Neville Plaice, Stephen Plaice, and Paul Knight. Cambridge, Mass.: MIT Press, 1986.
Burns, Bonnie. "*Dracula's Daughter:* Cinema, Hypnosis, and the Erotics of Lesbianism." In *Lesbian Erotics.* Ed. Karla Jay. New York: New York University Press, 1995. 196–211.
Calva Pratt, José Rafael. *Utopía gay.* Mexico City: Oasis, 1983.
Castle, Terry. *The Apparitional Lesbian: Female Homosexuality and Modern Culture.* New York: Columbia University Press, 1993.
Chávez Silverman, Suzanne. "The Look That Kills: The 'Unacceptable Beauty' of Alejandra Pizarnik's *La condesa sangrienta.*" In *¿Entiendes? Queer Readings, Hispanic Writings.* Ed. Emilie L. Bergmann and Paul Julian Smith. Durham: Duke University Press, 1995. 281–305.
Dorfman, Ariel. *The Last Song of Manuel Sendero.* Trans. George R. Shivers with the author. New York: Viking, 1987.
———. *La última canción de Manuel Sendero.* Mexico City: Siglo XXI, 1982.
Fernández, Sergio. *Los peces.* Mexico City: Joaquín Mortiz, 1968.
———. *Segundo sueño.* Mexico City: Joaquín Mortiz, 1976.
Finley, M. I. *The Use and Abuse of History.* New York: Penguin, 1987.
Frye, Northrop. "Varieties of Literary Utopias." *Daedalus* 94.2 (1965): 323–347.
Fuentes, Carlos. *Cambio de piel.* 1967. Barcelona: Seix Barral, 1974.
———. *A Change of Skin.* Trans. Sam Hileman. New York: Farrar, Straus and Giroux, 1968.
García Aguilar, Eduardo. "Final feliz para la literatura latinoamericana." *Sábado,* suplemento cultural de *unomásuno,* 26 julio 1987: 14.
Gorz, André. *Farewell to the Working Class: An Essay on Post-Industrial Socialism.* London: Pluto Press, 1982.
Hernández, Luisa Josefina. *Nostalgia de Troya.* Mexico City: Siglo XXI, 1970.
Khouri, Nadia. "The Politics of Utopia." Review of Jean Pfaelzer, *The Utopian Novel in America 1886–1896: The Politics of Form.* *Science-Fiction Studies* 14.41 (March 1987): 105–106.

Loaeza, Guadalupe. *Compro, luego existo.* 1992. Mexico City: Alianza Editorial, 1993.

Manuel, Frank, and Fritzie Manuel. *Utopian Thought in the Western World.* Cambridge, Mass.: Belknap Press of Harvard University Press, 1979.

Marcuse, Herbert. *Eros and Civilization: A Philosophical Inquiry into Freud.* Boston: Beacon, 1966.

Marin, Louis. *Utopics: Spatial Play.* Trans. Robert A. Vollrath. New Jersey: Humanities Press, 1984.

Monsiváis, Carlos. *Amor perdido.* Mexico City: Era, 1977.

More, Thomas. *Utopia.* 1551. New York: Knopf, 1992.

Moylan, Tom. *Demand the Impossible: Science Fiction and the Utopian Imagination.* New York: Methuen, 1986.

Owens, Craig. "The Discourse of Others: Feminists and Postmodernism." In *The Anti-Aesthetic: Essays on Postmodern Culture.* Ed. Hal Foster. Port Townsend, Wash.: Bay Press, 1983. 57–82.

Pizarnik, Alejandra. "The Bloody Countess." In *Other Fires: Short Fiction by Latin American Women.* Ed. Alberto Manguel. New York: C.N. Potter/Crown, 1986.

Quevedo, Francisco de. *La historia de la vida del Buscón.* Ed. Pablo Jauralde Pou. Madrid: Castalia, 1990.

Salazar, Severino. "Narrativa gay en México." *Opus Gay* 2 (1987): 10–12.

Tardanico, Richard. "Revolutionary Mexico and the World Economy: The 1920s in Theoretical Perspective." *Theory and Society* 13.6 (November 1984): 757–772.

Weiss, Andrea. *Vampires and Violets: Lesbians in the Cinema.* London: Cape, 1992.

Zapata, Luis. *Adonis García: A Picaresque Novel.* Trans. Edward A. Lacey. San Francisco: Gay Sunshine Press, 1981.

———. *Las aventuras, desventuras y sueños de Adonis García, el vampiro de la colonia Roma.* Mexico City: Grijalbo, 1979.

———. *En jirones.* Mexico City: Editorial Posada, 1985.

On the
Cutting Edge:
El jinete azul and
the Aesthetics
of the Abyss

Better to die from extremes than starting
from the extremities.
— Jean Baudrillard, *The Transparency of Evil*

Sadomasochism is only a noun.
— Robert J. Stoller, *Pain and Passion*

In mid-1991 José Rafael Calva wrote, in one of his frequent contributions to
the *sábado* (Saturday) supplement of the Mexican newspaper *unomásuno,* of
an experience he had with a group of friends on a gay beach along the mid-
Atlantic coast of the United States. Entitled "Barbie va a la playa" (Barbie goes
to the beach), his editorial column describes the orchestration and staging of
an elaborate camp wedding between two Ken and Steve dolls — the traditional
macho boyfriend and best friend of Cold War–era Barbie and her crowd —
both of which are dressed in drag. To set up this spectacular performance,
which draws a multitude of intrigued onlookers to the dunes, Calva noted the
similarities between such open expressions of gay culture in the United States
and in Mexico (albeit mentioning only Acapulco in the 1960s when referring
to the latter country). Careful to avoid praising the potential attributes of one
culture over another, the writer concluded that in all aspects but one there

are equal opportunities for gay men to express themselves on both sides of the border. He reassured his fellow Mexicans that "nuestro país, en cuanto a cultura gaya, no está en el subdesarrollo, a excepción quizá de la subcultura del culto al cuero y el sadomasoquismo" (our country, as far as gay culture is concerned, is not underdeveloped, with the possible exception of the leather subculture and the cult of sadomasochism) (Calva Pratt 1991, 7). The clear suggestion of uncoupling the gay community from any socioeconomic model of development versus underdevelopment imposed either from within or out-side, and any further discussion of specific details of the practices noted, are topics mentioned but postponed as subjects for future columns.[1]

Leaving aside for the moment any consideration of Calva's accuracy regard-ing these comparisons, it is nonetheless tempting to seize his statement on leather and bondage at face value and use it as a lens through which to focus on his problematical 1985 novella *El jinete azul* (The blue horseman). Yet to pro-pose so reductionist a reading of such a disturbing and suggestive text would erase many of the more subtle metaphorical implications it contains, while simultaneously creating a dangerous identification between authorial figure and narrative text. It is far too easy and superficial to dismiss *El jinete azul* as either the boastful memoirs of a Jeffrey Dahmer–like social "misfit" or sexual "pervert" who cannibalizes the objects of his affection,[2] or as some warped re-flection of Calva's own announced enthrallment with leather fetishes, which he himself sees as more "idiosyncratic" (Calva Pratt 1994, 15) than indicative of general cultural changes or "progress" in terms of alternative tastes. For while there is no doubt that such issues and preferences are included in the text, they are embedded in a narrative whose concerns are far greater than the sum of its individual parts and whose potential impact on a community's imagina-tion cannot be reduced to a simple accusation of gratuitous morbidity. At its core is a quest for limit experiences—for narrator and for reader alike—that surpass and explode the safety of bourgeois sexuality. Through a sort of de-regulation of the representation of passion as well as violence, and through a breaking down of the artificial limits between them, such a quest takes shape.[3]

To begin with, one might wonder why in 1985, when AIDS is already taking its toll on populations around the world and strategies born of panic have begun to arise against gay communities, Calva chooses to make his homo-sexual narrator a surgeon, a gifted one at that, who turns his skills to private explorations of human anatomy for his own ends and gratification. But, on second glance, perhaps the question turns out to be no question at all. When the medical establishment is stumped, on the one hand, by the advances of a new disease against which its arsenal of technological weapons fails, but is touted on the other as the source of any and all hope for a cure at the hands of the designated specialist, that is to say when the human body ceases to be the source of rapture or pleasure for an autonomous subject and becomes instead the battlefield of technology and social morality, then the art of the surgeon seems to be a logical point of return and reexamination. And because his theater of operations is none other than the human body — its surfaces and internal geographies — the scenarios in which flesh comes in contact with flesh as both lover and "patient" can be placed at center stage. It is then that the outer skin is peeled away to reach the inner life of the object (and subject), an experience of knowledge and self-knowledge not always accessible or successfully articulated.

From the first perspective, as the personal record of a so-called deviant human being, *El jinete azul* would merely join the ranks of the tabloids that blatantly and incessantly convert the images of gay men into demonized spectacles of unbridled violence and uncontrollable passions. In this sense, the text could be used by some readers merely to confirm an essentialist vision of the desires of gay men as pathological appetites that must be cleansed or purged from the social body. But, in that case, there would have to be a moral to the story to justify its telling in the first place; the fate of such a "criminal" would have to be linked, for example, to deviant family life, which is where the suggestion of a cure by example could begin. A society hostile to any form of difference, whether it be sexual, ethnic, intellectual, racial, or biological, feels the need to impose what Arthur and Marilouise Kroker refer to as "the will to purity" (1993, 13) on such "degenerate" acts and fantasies as those recounted by the narrator/stalker, even if this purported purity is a national fantasy of its own that never existed in actuality and never will. Or, more insidiously, a self-proclaimed modern and "tolerant" society might just ignore a text such as Calva's, giving it no space in book reviews, cutting off all polemical encounters with readers, and repressing its existence completely, at least in public. As far as critics go, this seems to be the case here. *El jinete azul* contains no such moral turn at the end, however. No sentence is passed on the characters, no condemnation or conviction of their acts enters the text at any point. Yet as Viegener points out, "The homosexual killer sits at the juncture of two great social obsessions, homosexuality and criminality" (105).

Hence, from an alternate perspective, *El jinete azul* presents from the out-set a series of issues whose repression (or "tolerance") cannot be taken lightly because this very act of submerging gives rise to the myths on which modern Western society is based. Why do certain scenarios of pain and violence play out uncensored and uncensored across the media on a daily basis while the performance of personal desires that might link pain and pleasure are called deviant and perverse? Why are the collective sadistic rituals of war presented as accepted conventions of the human community, while erotic rituals of the flesh, even if in the theaters of the imagination, are dismissed as evil and con-demned outright? How are meaning and value assigned to experience by the individual and by the society? And is it possible to turn the clinical gaze of sci-entific inquiry into a probing beneath the surface of social "politeness, hypoc-risy, and superstition" (Morris 227) to recover control over the human body in all of its passionate imperfection ("impurity")? In Hocquenghem's vision of double-faceted homosexual desire, rather than opting for the representation of an "ascent towards sublimation, the superego, and social anxiety," which would reproduce normative behavior and an internalized fear of desire, Calva explores instead "a descent towards the abyss of non-personalised and uncodi-fied desire" (95), which challenges unfailing submission to socially organized roles and identities. This descent — a "fall" from the grace of tolerance, per-haps? — is narrated by Keith Lawless, classical music devotee, ardent admirer of attractive young men, trained scientist, social libertarian, botanical naturalist, and joyous celebrant of an aesthetic of pain who at no time is ever seriously haunted by the ghost of "social anxiety."

The demand to relativize the concepts of virtue and criminality is estab-lished from the opening of the narrative through an epigraph taken from the writings of the well-known French political and sexual renegade D. A. F. de Sade, even before the surgeon begins his tale. His words are meant to produce ambiguity rather than moral certainty: "No hay acción que sea completamente virtuosa, como tampoco totalmente criminal; el valor de una acción depende del momento y de la geografía" (There is no action that is completely virtuous, as there is none totally criminal; the value of an action depends on the moment and the place) (7). Any intrinsic notion of "value," any automatically positive or negative charge, is to be removed from the space of the text, because each action must be judged only within the boundaries of the specific (narrative) time and place in which it occurs. This specificity of circumstance is made up of the core of the narrowing concentric circles formed by the United States, New York City, Forty-second Street, a particular apartment. So it is that the "I," as yet unnamed, juxtaposes on the first page references to the sadism of "the American way of life" with its holocausts, world wars, acts of terrorism, willful indifference to suffering, and political repression, and references to the apart ment he has set up as a closed-off, protected space for his "centro de experi-mentaciones eróticas" (center for erotic experiments) (8). Within the sealed environment of these rooms, he has modified what was formerly a radio broad-cast studio into a place of solace for lost souls who he feels otherwise would be devoured by the violent and uncaring jungle of the outside, which makes value judgments on the relative worthiness of its inhabitants and treats them with little or no equality as human beings. (The narrator finds this particularly true with regard to the medical treatment of homosexual men by doctors in pub-lic hospitals; they are either used as guinea pigs or ridiculed for their physical ailments, which are always attributed to their active sexuality.) The adoles-cents he stalks and brings back to his privileged space, in which "todo está permitido, todo puede hacerse, sólo que con refinamiento" (everything is per-mitted, everything can be done, as long as it is with refinement) (13), already "lost" as individuals to the impersonality of contemporary society, take part in rituals designed to produce in all participants the maximum intensity of pain and passion simultaneously, reuniting the body and soul the narrator con-cludes have been separated from one another in modern times. The narrator-participant once again contrasts the world of acquisition, production, and socially prescribed reproduction with the inner sanctum of nonreproductivity he has established, "con palabras y dinero" (with words and money) (8), as an alternative to the conventional concepts of morality and freedom he finds false. This utopian, self-made world is the only place in which the narrator feels at total liberty. Yet it is ironic that such a ghettoized representation appears in the text as the only alternative for homosexuality. Despite his numerous forays into the straight world, the narrator always returns to the apartment, where he removes the camouflage dress he has donned to walk among others, osten-sibly without being noticed. (As a matter of fact, he strips down to bare skin upon his return.) This nevertheless reverses a traditional categorization of the natural and the unnatural, marking the prescribed appearance and behavior of the outside as the "abnormal" and thereby rendering the abstract moralizing of representational codes as relative and suspect in the process.

Strongly suggesting that he hastened along the death of his mother in order to inherit the extensive family fortune, the narrator leaves his medical work in the morgue at New York's infamous Bellevue Psychiatric Hospital to learn and practice the traditional art of herbal pharmacology at home. The erotic pleasure he finds, and proposes to offer others, in administering balms and healing ointments with caresses to those he himself has tortured and wounded, drives away any image of objective medical science and produces in its place the recovery of a subjective experience of the body. The discourse on his methods of operation also aestheticizes pain, both its source and its cure. No blood flows from any cut, every move is done with precision and without wasted motion, and the responsive flesh of the human body is described in exquisite and loving detail in order to preserve every instant of shared passion. Both the cause and effect of each act are subsumed within the Sadeian aesthetic of the narrator in his carefully orchestrated calculations; nothing is left to chance, but instead all is patiently planned. On the contrary, the process of self-recognition on the part of Richard, his initiation into a cult of adoration toward the male body (including his own), is a cautiously recounted series of steps with this, his first, lover. The actual distance between the two men is closed along with the door of the apartment, their physical contact is sensual and prolonged, Keith is solicitous of the other's pleasure even to the point of tenderly spoiling him like "una orquídea del Amazonas" (an Amazonian orchid) (14) and worshiping his youth and virility: "comprendí el gozo secreto que exuda la madre tierra en su húmedo perfume cuando recibe la lluvia de la tarde en un verano caluroso" (I understood the secret delight that Mother Earth exudes in her humid perfume when she receives the afternoon rain during a parched summer) (18–19). None of this highly aestheticized desire reflects any hint of a lack of control in its premeditation and precise narration, a process Lawless describes as the rigorous practice of self-control, "un ejercicio de ascesis para alcanzar la perfección" (an exercise in self-restraint in order to reach a state of perfection) (18). In his view, only the path of rigorous self-discipline, a recovery of power over the self, will lead Keith to the ecstasy of passion and fulfillment.

Since the reader has been warned already to set down no abstract grid of values over these scenes, to draw no battle lines between good and evil, the categories of innocence and monstrosity are placed in question constantly throughout the text. After ten erotic encounters and ten rituals of dismemberment, Keith Lawless wonders, just this one time, what others would think of him if they knew what he had done. It is not a thought he has entertained — or allowed himself to entertain — before. In legal and moral terms he figures he would be considered a criminal (16), but just where does such a sense of traditional morality fit in with his aesthetics? Is Lawless's avowed "ciclo de amor cerrado e infalible" (closed and infallible cycle of love) (33) as utopian as nineteenth-century English writer Thomas De Quincey's 1827 essay "On Murder Considered as One of the Fine Arts," in which this act is removed from all moral realms and cast instead in terms of the beauty of its execution? While actual instances of social violence are presented to the public regularly and in their own way "artistically," tamed by the popular media through the processes of editing, cutting, and focusing, then what can be said of this character's subjective experiences? The audience's possible excitement over and titillation by the one (mediated version of events) can still lead to a condemnation of the other (so-called unmediated acts related by an individual), culminating in a sublimation or censoring of any pleasurable feelings possibly provoked by certain spectacles of violence. Or the unmediated confession of the human "monster" already presumed guilty can serve as a restoration of social order as long as its contents are perceived as imagined threats to so-called decent everyday life (which nevertheless always triumphs in the end). Any attraction or pleasure connected with the aberrant "case" must be suspended to reach such a satisfactory conclusion, needless to say, for identification would be seen as breeding anarchy.

The only arena permitted and even condoned by society for the gruesome exaggeration and exploitation of these feelings is tabloid (yellow) journalism. *Alarma!* and, since 1986, *El nuevo Alarma! Unicamente la verdad,* displayed and sold at virtually all sidewalk kiosks in Mexico, make no distinction between the categories of political, economic, or sexual violence included in their issues, and use graphic language and lurid photographic "evidence" to drive home their stories, which culture critic Medina has said are thereby made to appear as "uncontested realities" (27). (In other words, what the picture is interpreted as becomes the actual reality of the scene.) Spectacles of dismembered bodies, crimes of passion, transvestites detained by the police, molested children, victims of drunk drivers, and brutal thieves all share the same space on the front page. But so do people with born with birth defects, hirsute so-called wolf-men, Siamese twins, and even a report of the government-sponsored massacre in Tlatelolco in an issue from 1968. Among all these bodies of forensic evidence, the relationship between the solid ground of good and the shifting terrain of evil is never placed in doubt. One is led to ask, then, which set of depictions seems more uncontrollable and diabolical, those of the popular press or those of Keith Lawless with his plan to rescue the body and its passions from the realm of inarticulateness and anonymity? Is he wresting the human body away from those who have sought to control it, letting the flesh speak for itself instead of being interpreted and presented by others? By frequently using metaphorical language to describe his sexual encounters and to heighten the atmosphere of affect, and by exhibiting an expert's acquaintance-ship with classical music as an accompaniment to his disarticulation of human bodies, the narrator produces a much more ambiguous representation of his personality and activities. He simultaneously points to the fact that all texts—tabloids included—*represent* violence in forms much more regulated (mediated) than even the violent acts themselves. In this way, Lawless suggests the power of the media as being greater than that of one individual over another at any particular moment or in any given scenario. The same could be said, of course, of images of homosexual desire and how the public is taught to read them. The linkage of homosexuality with crime in tabloid reporting is often the only representation made available to the general public, resulting in a conflation of the demonic and the erotic.

As Joel Black argues with regard to the representation of violent acts such as murder, "By suppressing or denying our aesthetic experiences, we create a moral 'reality' that is, in fact, our supreme fiction. This grand artifice or ideology of moral reason can only maintain itself as Truth at the continued expense of the individual's own subjective feelings, his or her aesthetic and erotic responses to the world" (4). Calva's text recognizes this fact a priori, and de-mythologizes the feigned innocence with which collective social horrors are perpetrated, by making the reader an accomplice to acts conventionally censored as monstrously horrible in the general schema of society and by inverting conventional categories. Lawless's adventures are presented here calmly as part of a microcosmic world in which desire has much more effect than it does in the "outside" world, which is governed by a fear of desire (all the while knowing of its existence, however—a fact to which the tabloids and popular media so often attest). Careful to maintain his appearance on the street as a "tímido caballero" (timid gentleman) (16) going about his daily business, Lawless nevertheless rejects any hint of a Jekyll-Hyde split in favor of a single personality with no inherent inconsistencies or contradictions. This holds true whether he strolls among superficial and dehumanized inhabitants of the metropolis who are incapable of seeing him for what he really is (a man perhaps more like others than they might admit or, as Lawless says, "Sin lugar a dudas tengo la apariencia de muchos y cualquiera puede ser como yo" [Without a shadow of a doubt my appearance is just like that of many others and anyone can be like me] [17]), or performs his ceremonies in the climate-controlled environment of his apartment. He declares "soy siempre el mismo" (I'm always one and the same) (17), a man in search of aesthetic perfection, a utopian personal freedom, and an open and honest recognition of what gives him pleasure. He ingests no processed foods, imbibes no toxin-laden drinking water, wears no synthetic clothing (he goes naked in the Eden-like seventy-five-degree warmth of the building), and rediscovers his own body in the absolute possession of those he seduces with a passion that "un dólar no puede comprar, . . . una guerra no resuelve, . . . una revolución no conquista" (a dollar can't buy, . . . a war doesn't resolve, . . . a revolution doesn't win) (26). In other words, Lawless rejects what he calls the egocentric bellicosity of neocapitalist society in favor of a more libidinal economy of his own. Compared with the perversity of a false collective innocence constructed on willful ignorance or moral self-justification, the narrator finds his own vision of the world more honest and innocent because he attempts to hide none of the motivations behind his acts. The one and only force behind them is an uncompromising impulse toward ecstasy guided by his readings of the Spanish mystic Saint John of the Cross and the already-mentioned Marquis de Sade, exemplary individuals he feels arrived at a similar dynamic fusion of spirit and flesh, albeit by different—if equally ascetic and ecstatic—routes.[4]

It is the virtue accorded the middle class's sentimentalizing of relationships and romanticizing of the human body that Lawless rejects as for him truly grotesque and monstrous.[5] When he meets Richard, the tenth of his victims and the one object of desire capable of provoking the narration of this tale, he looks for some sign of difference, and not just a reenactment of storybook perfection, in their mutual attraction. He asks in retrospect, as he simultaneously dissects the cadaver and the encounter: "¿Por qué no cometías un error, uno

siquiera? Todo era tan clasemedieramente romántico . . . sólo faltaba que me
pusiera a leer *Sonnets of the Portuguese* [sic] con voz aterciopelada y que nos
hiciéramos juramentos de amor eterno" (Why didn't you make a mistake, just
one? Everything was so middle-classly romantic . . . the only thing missing was
my reading *Sonnets of the Portuguese* [sic] with a velvety voice and our swear-
ing undying love for each other) (19). In the perfection of his moment of death
and/at orgasm, that instant frozen in Richard's eyes and Keith's memory, their
brief but intense encounter of two weeks is turned into an unrepeatable paradigm of possession and pleasure for the narrator, so much so that he confesses
to the corpse that he laments "que sólo hayas podido morir una vez" (that
you were only capable of dying once) (11). But in that single moment time is
held at bay and beauty—the aesthetic of Hocquenghem's "descent toward the
abyss of uncodified desire"—is preserved at its peak, before love turns to hate
or possession turns to loss or youthful flesh shows the marks of age or disease.
While the remainder of his sacrificial acts have fortified his own ego, a shifting
conjunction of Eros and Thanatos being the single distinguishing practice of
identity he finds possible in the stifling anonymity and homogeneity of capitalist society, Richard's death at the hands of his lover brings out in him the
sentiment Lawless most rejects. He admits to himself (and by extension to the
reader) that he misses Richard, that nostalgia is taking over his feelings, that
he senses not regret but loss: "Después de todo es triste. Algo jamás antes sen-
tido" (After all it's sad. Something I never felt before) (10), "Te juro, nadie
me había hecho llorar con su memoria" (I swear, no one's memory had ever
made me cry) (39). Could he have done otherwise and kept Richard alive in
order to preserve their conjunction of libidinal energy? Such an alternative to
death seems impossible, since it would have risked their separation (already
rehearsed when Richard left the apartment one evening, only to be drawn
back into it the next) or a change in their relationship (a "mistake" or devia-
tion from the master plan, as Keith had tried to find earlier) between perfect
slave and obsessed master, two scenarios Lawless finds inevitable. Therefore,
Richard has to cease existing, to materially disappear, before the perfect moment becomes contaminated by time or remorse or analysis.

   In choosing the instant and disposition of death, both Richard's and his
own, the narrator claims for himself the last act of freedom accorded any
human being. Before either one becomes a victim of the North American economic system, which is presented as devouring human flesh and repressing

bodily instincts, converting working bodies into wealth and profit for others (as in the case of his father's own vast fortune), Lawless turns that metaphor of consumption into a literal act of revenge. He ritually ingests the flesh of the men he lures to his rooms, a "savage" (38) in the Garden of Eden of his cloistered space. But these acts are also preemptive strikes against the ritualized dehumanization of a society that imposes its rigid laws of production and reproduction on its members. He devours them before he becomes a victim. As a social human being, "Lawless" is not absolutely without laws, nevertheless. Rather, his deeds serve as an example of activities that are seen to require laws to keep them in check; an "ascent" into laws is the flip side of a "descent" into desires. Though it is easy to equate the mutilated bodies with the work of recent serial killers such as Wisconsin's Dahmer, who continues both to intrigue and to repel modern society, even after death, Keith Lawless's arguments point in other directions. His contention that massive human sacrifices have been made in order to put beef on the table of the country's wealthy prompts his actual consumption of the bodies of his "guests." He tells Richard that "No sólo carne humana [has comido]. Carne de norteamericanos homosexuales: el secreto de la vida eterna, una forma ritual de autofagia" ([You haven't eaten] just human flesh. The flesh of North American homosexuals: the secret of eternal life, a ritual form of devouring the self) (38), thereby bringing to the surface what Lawless considers a ritual act of survival and self-affirmation. Rather than becoming invisible, a vampire whose tenuous existence wavers on the fine line between death and periodic revival, Lawless with his fantasies remains part of the life of the mainstream. He shuns the ghettoized spaces carefully set aside for gay encounters—the city's underground bars, nightclubs and back rooms, public bathrooms in Grand Central Station, Fire Island bungalows—where the repressed is permitted to surface under strict ostracism and control. He favors instead the bourgeois scenarios that best promote an "ascent into sublimation and social anxiety." (One might find a logical aesthetic parallel in Calva's shunning of the tabloid format, except as covert reference, and his preference for the more erudite genre of the novella as a territory to be usurped and conquered for itself by these narratives of alterity.) Such invaded spaces include Bloomingdale's, Park Avenue, and the Cathedral of Saint John the Divine where, during the celebration of the body and blood of Christ in the Eucharist, the surgeon begins his furtive quest to commune with the body of Richard. As if the two spaces—of ascent and descent—were separable and mutually exclusive! In Hocquenghem's radical theory of the subject, the legalized venues of (heterosexual) pleasure and the criminal or pathological (nonsublimated homosexuality) are two sides of the same coin, present concurrently and interwoven into the social fabric much more than even the "will to purity" would have it. The greater the insistence on collective cleansing and on the imposition of the disciplinary "law" over the extensive and inexhaustible realm of libidinal possibilities, the more the canons of legality are forced to occupy a shifting terrain with diabolical desire or, as Paul Julian Smith (following Foucault) concludes, "power carries resistance within it, . . . discipline both polices and produces the territories of homosexual affect" (9). One might even be tempted to argue that Keith Lawless is the exquisitely perfect—and aptly monstrous for that very reason—embodiment of the coexistence of desublimated desire *and* a literal cleansing of society as he cleans up after himself. As the narrator recounts, Richard and the others before him "han entrado a mi casa por la puerta y han salido por la tubería de agua negra" (have entered my house through the door and exited through the sewer system) (9). In a literal sense, their bodies and excretions are broken down into their most elemental components and returned to nature through the infrastructure built by society for that very purpose. But in a more figurative sense the "surgical compulsion" (Baudrillard 45) to excise the rejected, or to remodel it into idealized forms if at all possible, demands the removal of all traces of contamination from the scene of the crime. What has been present in the flesh, as it were, must be returned to the subterranean depths, much as Lawless feels compelled to leave the room when Richard's material body begins to decompose in order to be able to conjure him up (alive and not malodorous) from a distance, where the stench of reality doesn't mar his nostalgic evocations.

Just as scenes of violence or passion are processed by the media to blur the details or eliminate any "rough edges" that the audience—or some undetermined portion of it—might be tempted to examine more closely, the surgeon uses all the means at his disposal to sterilize the space of his previous encounters. What society has taught him now serves his own purposes. Along with the bloodless penetration of the beloved's chest by the phallic Toledo steel blade, this cleansing is part of his "art" and the greatest point of distinction between tragic tabloid gore and literary aesthetics. The only remaining vestiges of the precarious moment between life and death linger in the imagination of the narrator, who reveals the details after the fact in the manner of an autopsy of the acts he has committed. The Greek root of the term *autopsy*, however, means to see with one's own eyes. And what the reader already has been drawn into, what he or she has witnessed, is something ordinarily sealed off from probing eyes — something deemed so loathsome by society that there are no words to describe it. (We might remember that, in its various incarnations, *Alarma!* has depended on screaming headlines and grainy photographs to catch the eye of the consumer; careful, dispassionate, and objective reporting of events is neither its strong point nor its aim.) But Keith Lawless never seems to be at a loss for language, and the one thing he admonishes Richard for is his silence (36), his inability to articulate any reaction to the scenarios taking place in the counterworld of Lawless's apartment. The reader's acquaintance with the narrated acts creates a complicity with the story's actors, what Joel Black refers to as "an erotic bond of shared knowledge" (107), whether any pleasure derived is resublimated or not. The intimacy created between storyteller and listener (reader) is similar to that shared by the voyeur and the exhibitionist, each of whom depends on the other to fulfill a pacted role. Lawless finds a similar tacit "agreement" in Richard's willing participation in their sexual encounters. He addresses the following remarks to the cadaver of his last lover: "Tú pediste tu cautivero, tu sumisión. Inocentemente, te prestaste a tu secuestro" (You asked for your own captivity, your submission. You innocently lent yourself to your own abduction) (12). The surgeon and his victim are cast in their roles accordingly, as if brought together in this human laboratory by fate or destiny.

Yet Lawless's skills are learned, and they are transmissible to others such as Leo, the young novice and proxy for Richard to whom Keith wishes to submit his own body at the end of the story, those specifically chosen to continue practicing his "art." Such intimacy, between reader and narrator or between objects of affection, is set up through a discourse not meant to rationalize but to liberate the performances that are executed in the name of artistry and desire in the midst of a world of violent and judgmental mediocrity and conformity. While Lawless laments the lack of communication in his victim, who expires mutely if not dispassionately, he imbues his own acts with a greater symbolic meaning. He states: "más habla de la libertad la posibilidad de hundir mi bisturí en este hombro para separar el brazo del tórax de Richard que miles de pancartas que se envanecen de una liberación *gay*, porque mi libertad va más allá de seguir patrones de conducta" (the possibility of plunging my scalpel into this shoulder to separate Richard's arm from his thorax says more about freedom than do thousands of placards and posters that vainly proclaim gay liberation, because my freedom goes way beyond following [established] models of behavior) (8–9). Because his actions speak even louder than words, according to both his own interpretation and that of society, and because no moment can be repeated except as a pale simulacrum of a previous epiphany, once Lawless decides to orchestrate his own death and join Richard, pleasure, pain, and (narrative) language fuse in one last anticipated event. It is a given for the narrator that no one of these components can survive the others, because he is the crucial link among them. Narration accompanies his every action, which relies in turn on language to be preserved.

The celebratory discourse of sadomasochism underlying *El jinete azul* represents Hocquenghem's dual schema on another level as well. Its "descent" into the insistent fantasies of Keith Lawless is counterbalanced by a simultaneous "ascent" into a genre of literary acceptability: it is a novella published by a "reputable" and recognized company. Although some critics offered backhanded praise of the first edition of his previous novel *Utopía gay* (Gay utopia),[6] citing its firm anchorage in the realm of the biological and medical absurd and its consequent harmlessness—in the words of one, the text is "*limpiamente* absurdo" (*cleanly* absurd) (Cohen 83), attesting to the idea that it is neither yellow (tabloid), pink (sentimental, erotic), nor blue (pornographic) but somehow colorless—there exists to this day no review, no mention, of *El jinete azul* in the Mexican press or elsewhere. Perhaps this is because it can no longer be judged so "clean" a text; it cannot be concluded that "No recurre a feísmos, no pretende escandalizar las buenas conciencias con escenas de gloriosa depravación a todo color con jadeos y sangre y *guagüis* a la intemperie" (It doesn't resort to nasty scenes, it doesn't pretend to scandalize pious dogooders with technicolor scenes of glorious depravation complete with heavy breathing and blood and sex out in the open) (Cohen 83), as was written about *Utopía gay.* It appears instead as if with this text Calva has taken on the challenge of defying the repressive language used in the above quote to do exactly the opposite of what was deemed acceptable and inoffensive about his other work, and by doing so to place in question the solemnity of many conventional attitudes accepted, without hesitation, on a daily basis. This would include the denial of the violent and sensual fantasies of the "timid gentleman" Keith Lawless, who reminds us repeatedly that he is no exception to the human race, no member of a so-called third gender, but indeed just like anyone else who is driven to resist repressive social cleansing and control. The fact is that while others submissively conform to prescribed patterns of acceptable behavior, Lawless submits himself totally and passionately to his libido. If everyone were to follow suit, in his view they would open up the narrow space to which the law assigns desire. To exemplify this possibility, the narrator chooses a literary and, later, cinematic icon of patriarchal order: Mr. Chips, schoolmaster extraordinaire and "healthy" figure of (heterosexual) desire. Yet Lawless reaches into the hidden recesses of this hero to bring out what he believes to be a repressed affinity between them. He concludes that "El intachable Mr. Chips puede hundir un puñal en la vagina de su novia y decirle 'te amo' mientras ella muere para que en lugar de morir gritando ella muera besándolo, para dejar su vida en los labios del maestro" (The irreproachable Mr. Chips can plunge a knife into the vagina of his lover and tell her 'I love you' as she expires so that instead of dying with screams on her lips she does so while covering him with kisses, leaving her life on the lips of her teacher) (17–18). The extremity of such an act, in this case performed by a man on a woman but equally by men on other men in passages contained elsewhere in the text, is most certainly not unproblematical. Yet in both instances the phenomena imagined and described once again conjoin the censure of the community and the revolt of the individual subject in one moment of potential autonomy and singularity. The delusion of unity (the illusion of a clean or cleansed Mr. Chips and his pupils) is ruptured for a split second to allow for a vision of difference, of excess; it is indicative of a "descent" from the watchtower of social anxiety into the abyss of sheer ego.

So it is that Prince Charming, the heroic man on the white steed, the object of lifelong desire, has now become "El jinete azul" or the *blue* knight of an imagination pushed to the limits. As such he becomes the epitome of pornography—a discourse in blue—in the eyes of "decent" society and a parody of the discourse of correction and rectification found in sensationalist crime tabloids and other disciplinary texts. Far from being subjected to a collectively sanctioned and imposed punishment of any type whatsoever, Keith Lawless chooses his own ending to the story he tells: closure of the narrative and closure of his life take place in a moment of ecstatic pleasure, not societal imposition. In the narrator's own words, "no hay nada en mi pasado de lo que desee arrepentirme" (there is nothing in my past for which I might wish to repent) (18). After all, it is clear that the act of repentance belongs to a category from the realm of morality, not of aesthetics.

Moreover, it has been established already that Lawless has formulated his personal space as an isolated haven for any and all sexual activity he might desire to experience, with one mandated exclusion: "la única excepción [es] de [tener relaciones con] una mujer, porque eso va en contra mis principios de sexo no productivo, basado en la idea de que mi sexo está sólo para delei-tarme" (the only exception [is having relations with] a woman, since that goes against my principles of nonreproductive sex, based on the idea that my sex organ is there only to give me pleasure) (9). He also has renounced pro-ductive work as a member of the medical establishment to dedicate his days and nights to another sort of healing, one that produces no financial remu-neration but exquisite personal satisfaction. With such a willful assumption of the mask of "degeneracy" — as Hocquenghem proposes, "the homosexual can only be [seen by heterosexual society as] a degenerate, for he does not gen-erate" (107) — Keith Lawless irreparably rends the social fabric of an everyday life premised on and supported by productivity and material utility (capitalist production, accumulation, and surplus value). His existence, one that haunts the social body and need be relegated permanently to the shadowy realm of the repressed, embodies a resounding refusal to respect limits. As Bataille has written, "The goal of [material utility] is, theoretically, pleasure — but only in a moderate form, since violent pleasure is seen as pathological" (116). It would be logical to surmise, then, that the flaunting of "violent pleasure" or plea-surable — blue — violence demands more from society than the moderation of affect it is willing to allow any given individual. In other words, Lawless seizes with both hands more than his allotted share and he returns nothing useful to the collectivity. It is the "irrationality" or immoderation of his consumption, a literal act of absorption and material disappearance in the case of his lovers, that could be most thoroughly condemned by society. Yet by making the narrator Lawless a spectacle of excess, a gloriously articulate but stunningly voracious example of Bataille's concept of "unreproductive expenditure" (118), Calva places other instances of such expenditure under scrutiny as well. This includes acts of war, the arts (including literature), luxury, cults, and "perverse sexual activity" (Bataille 118). At this point we might return with renewed interest to the first page of *El jinete azul* to reconsider the narrator's introduc-tory argument centered on the sadistic cruelty of the "neocapitalist hedonism" of the United States (7). Could a spectacular display of power exercised over others as an end in itself — a display coldly indifferent to all consequences but justified in its media versions — be seen as anything but an ideological repre-sentation when included as part of the monologues of Keith Lawless, a man whose own practices are merely part of an ongoing dialogue with society's moral imperatives?

Notes

1   One recent example of a return to these issues appears in his repudiation of a gay Mexican's recent request for political asylum in the United States under the category of refugee from sexual persecution in his own country. The INS's granting of this request in early 1994 leads Calva to compare the codified and institutionalized homophobia of the United States with what he calls a more tolerant attitude in Mexico toward gays, both historically and in contemporary society. (Calva Pratt 1994, 15). For the potential dangers of "tolerance," however, see José Joaquín Blanco 1991, 293–296.

2   I have purposely set off the adjectives "misfit" and "pervert" in quotes because these terms form the basis of both legal and moral discussions of the Dahmer case and its prosecution, in the gay press and elsewhere. The fifteen — later seventeen — murders of which he was accused, and to which he ultimately confessed, victimized young men, frequently of Asian, African-American, or Hispanic descent, picked up in gay bars. Dahmer's admission of a certain compulsion (the word is his) to cruise the streets and of a drive to mutilate and cannibalize his victims compounded the "law's" views on the case. Dahmer is not merely another in the string of serial killers appearing over the past several decades; his motives are seen as belonging to the criminal characterization of the (homo)sexual and therefore even more problematic.

This situation was evident from the outset when Dahmer pleaded "innocent by reason of mental defect," then this was changed to "not guilty by reason of insanity," and finally "guilty" but insane. The questioning of his mental capacity — a gay man driven by a "mental defect" that somehow went along with his sexual preference — posited the possibility of homosexuality as the sole culprit of these crimes. The "horrors" of which potential jurors were warned were committed by someone outside the realm of the lawful, the normal, and the sane — by definition, a "misfit," a "deviant," and therefore his actions confirmed this diagnosis as a self-fulfilling prophecy of his character. This was the battle waged across the pages of the press, complicated in many instances by texts filled with the details of dismemberment alongside pictures of Dahmer with his parents. It is unclear whether this juxtaposition was intended to show that the family was the social unit guilty of provoking his actions or to prove that appearances do not necessarily reveal the "dark side" of the social body. Its effect was to do both at once.

For the approximately two-month duration of the trial, evidence was presented to prove that Dahmer, as the court-appointed psychiatrist concluded, was "sick but not psychotic," was "legally sane" but driven to kill by a compulsion to have sex (with men). (This was the argument sustained by the defense as well.) Since he could have chosen not to kill at any time, according to this theory, Dahmer's "sickness" must have been what prevented him from making that rational decision. Therefore, his homosexuality (repressed or not) must have been the cause of his acts. But the case became even more complicated, and the ambiguity of the "law" was shown clearly, when members of the Milwaukee Police Department were criticized for their complicity in at least one of the murders. By arresting, but then releasing, Dahmer and another young man—who pleaded for help after fleeing from Dahmer's apartment—after concluding that the latter's nudity and expression of terror were just "normal" aspects of a relationship between two men, they provided the scenario for another of Dahmer's ritualistic killings. The debates provoked by this case, even after the defendant's death in prison at the hands of another inmate, continue to play out in the press.

3   Only recently did I run across a reprinted paperback, originally published in 1968, that is so suggestive of Calva's text that it begs to be mentioned at this time. Despite the uncertainty of their actual relationship as antecedent and reinterpretation or as source and inspired reading, the strong similarities between William Carney's *The Real Thing* and José Rafael Calva's *El jinete azul* are certainly worth exploring in some detail.

   Carney's text is composed of a series of epistolary entries from an uncle to a long-silent nephew who has, seemingly out of the blue after a fifteen-year absence, inquired about "the Way" of sadomasochism. The unnamed uncle is presented as an adept in what he himself refers to as the "higher calling" (20) of the fine (erotic) arts to which this community within the society at large is dedicated. Both the terminology used to describe their activities as religious ritual behavior—references to "conversions" (15, 21), "initiates" (23), "benedictions" (23), and so on, abound—and the insistence on disciplined activity that leads to an ascent into the "perfect" order of master-slave logically might lead one to conclude that Calva's surgeon-turned-healer Keith Lawless is the embodiment of the leathermen for whom this narrator speaks. (Or, rather, of whom he writes—for in this text the urge to narrate in vivid detail the experiences of a lifetime of practice is sparked by the nephew's inquiring letters, which prick the ego of the uncle and inspire him to reveal his secrets.)

   From the outset, the uncle/narrator sets the tone of the story as information to be taken seriously. This is the "real thing," he reiterates, not playing at being sadists and masochists. It means espousing a way of life elaborated according to a code, a set of rules, an a priori agreement as to each participant's role. The downfalls, as it were, of both Keith Lawless and the relationship between uncle and nephew, are hinted at in this expert's discussion of two types of response to the practices described. He spells out their possibilities as well as their risks: "Reaction on the moral (unconscious) plane presents a much greater danger to the community than does the same reaction sustained physically and consciously" (14). That is to say, the individual might be faithful to the pleasurable practices of the flesh without internalizing the fundamental challenge to traditional social morality implied by the philosophical system in place behind such acts. The "discipline" of which he writes, then, is both physical and moral, giving in neither to sentimentality nor to superficial relationships but maintaining instead a "taxonomy of the world" (14) based on daily training and a "system of knowledge" (61) inaccessible to "outsiders." Just as Richard is not the run-of-the-mill victim but is imbued (posthumously) with special qualities by Lawless, so does the nephew end up in the thrall of "received sentimental morality" (51) when he uses the lessons of his uncle to take revenge. This is not part of the "pact." The "master" is done in through his own teachings by this younger brother of a former "slave," both of whom just happen to be the older man's nephews as well.

Calva's Lawless is a man of science, a surgeon integrated into that special brotherhood of medical initiates whose expertise is highly valued by society in general and by the cult of sadomasochism in particular. The sobriety of his rituals, the precision of his acts, and his knowledge of anatomy reflect what Carney's narrator calls the perfect "mode of observation and controlled experimentation" (60) to which the scientist has access. The religiosity of medical practices, the belief in their power, are also reflected in the uncle, whose identity as an academic is revealed early on (16). He is an expert, a teacher, the perfect instructional vehicle for the eager nephew. And his total adherence to his art is exemplary: "He is devoted to the task of breaking the victim he confronts in the manner of the priest who creases and splits the host. He contemplates his victim, worshipping him with studied savagery, and the victim, broken, is consumed" (31). One could hardly invent a more perfect concordance between the stalking of the adored prey by Lawless and the moments of transcendental ecstasy described repeatedly by Carney's narrator. Across the three motivating facets of vision, will, and technique (30) outlined in *The Real Thing*, the two characters seem to tread each other's footsteps along the road to perfection.

Neither man has rejected outright the world around him, but each has instead sought ways to survive amid its ruins. The uncle tells his young disciple, "I have embraced the world in order to extract from it what I need" (61); their relationship with things surrounding them is on their own terms and not in accordance with the dictates of "common and sentimental attachments" (55) such as family. Yet the concept of the familial haunts both texts: the wealth of his father in Lawless's case provides

the means to live as he chooses; the evils of the nephew's mother and the "community of blood" (20), who have tried to make him into "a moral cripple and a social
reject" (58) motivate the acts of the uncle/narrator. It is curious how often there are
references to the family in each, however, despite the protests of the two narrators
to the contrary. When the uncle, castrated by a "master" of his own creation, ap-
peals to his nephew's "family solidarity" and sense of "decency" (148) to finish off
the job he has begun, the language is as disturbing as the recourse to surgical skills
used by the master-turned-victim. The artistry performed on the body of the victim in this case is imperfect, the work is incomplete, the science of life and death is
left in limbo because the uncle is alive but "useless" to others of his persuasion as he
himself so eloquently states. The only way to complete the scenario is to play to the
residual sympathies of the would-be executioner, draw him into a trap by means of
the very weaknesses he ought to have cast out, and kill his nephew in an "excruciat-
ing, protracted, agonizing, perfect" (151) act. And this is exactly what Carney uses
to end the tale. Lawless is by no means far removed from a similar closure, however, in his plan to instruct a young man in the arts he has so perfected in order to
orchestrate his own ritualized death at the hands of an ardent admirer/convert. The
crossovers between spiritual and physical desire, and the carefully detailed narration of the two parallel worldviews, make each of these texts a fascinating comple-
ment to the other with much remaining to be explored between them.

4   Lawless also mentions that his library includes works by the following "grandes
alucinados" (great visionaries) (26) as well: Poe, De Quincey, Dostoievski, Sacher-
Masoch, Camus, and Genet. One might wonder whether Yukio Mishima's novels
Confessions of a Mask and *Forbidden Colors,* or Spanish novelist Juan Goytisolo's
Paisajes después de la batalla (Scenes after the battle) wouldn't qualify as texts by
similarly "deluded visionaries." Mishima's aestheticized act of ritual public suicide
and Goytisolo's homonymous Reverend (a Parisian version of Lewis Carroll, the
literary alias of *Alice in Wonderland's* author Charles L. Dodgson), who establishes
a secret apartment in the heart of the city from which he ventures forth—at least in
his imagination—to fantasize plagues, invasions, exhibitionism, and the seduction
of young girls to help satisfy his own masochism, seem prime material for Lawless's collection. It goes without saying that the works of Georges Bataille also merit
consideration, since many of their fundamental ideas—the concept of excess, the
notion of expenditure, etc.—would seem to underlie Calva's novella (see Bataille,
116–129).

5   Such hyperbolic sentiments are explored in less carnivorous terms in the short
stories that make up the collection *Variaciones y fuga sobre la clase media* (Variations and fugue on the middle class), in which each tale portrays a failed human
relationship and the false grounds on which it had been established in the first

place. Published five years before *El jinete azul,* this anthology might be considered to represent the society of comfortable illusions against which Lawless takes concerted action.

6   In a recent newspaper column Calva mentions that he has prepared a new edition of this novel, including a second prologue and a new ending, to be published by an unnamed editorial house in the near future. No further details of the project are given. His mention of this project appears as part of a discussion of all the cultural and literary activities he has undertaken since finding out he is HIV-positive. (See Calva Pratt 1993, 31).

Works Cited

Bataille, Georges. "The Notion of Expenditure." In *Visions of Excess: Selected Writings, 1927–1939.* Ed. Allan Stoekl. Trans. Allan Stoekl with Carl R. Lovitt and Donald M. Leslie, Jr. Minneapolis: University of Minnesota Press, 1985. 116–129.

Baudrillard, Jean. *The Transparency of Evil: Essays on Extreme Phenomena.* Trans. James Benedict. London: Verso, 1993.

Black, Joel. *The Aesthetics of Murder: A Study in Romantic Literature and Contemporary Culture.* Baltimore: Johns Hopkins University Press, 1991.

Blanco, José Joaquín. "Eyes I Dare Not Meet in Dreams." Trans. Edward A. Lacey. In *Gay Roots: Twenty Years of Gay Sunshine.* Ed. Winston Leyland. San Francisco: Gay Sunshine Press, 1991. 291–296.

Calva Pratt, José Rafael. "Anticrónica: Visita a México." *unomásuno* 30 junio 1993: 31.

———. "Barbie va a la playa." *Sábado,* suplemento cultural de *unomásuno,* 25 julio 1991: 7.

———. *El jinete azul.* Mexico City: Katún, 1985.

———. "¿Migración *gay*? Así se escribe la historia." *Sábado,* suplemento cultural de *unomásuno,* 30 abril 1994: 15.

———. *Utopía gay.* Mexico City: Editorial Oasis, 1983.

———. *Variaciones y fuga sobre la clase media.* Xalapa: Universidad Veracruzana, 1980.

Carney, William. *The Real Thing.* 1968. New York: Richard Kasak, 1995.

Cohen, Sandro. "*Utopía gay:* que nadie se ofenda." *Casa del Tiempo* 3.31/32 (julio/agosto 1983): 82–83.

Goytisolo, Juan. *Paisajes después de la batalla.* Barcelona: Montesinos, 1982.

Hocquenghem, Guy. *Homosexual Desire.* Trans. Daniella Dangoor. 1972. Durham: Duke University Press, 1993.

Kroker, Arthur, and Marilouise Kroker, eds. *The Last Sex: Feminism and Outlaw Bodies.* New York: St. Martins, 1993.

Medina, Cuauhtémoc. "*Alarma!* Crimen y circulación/*Alarma!* Crime and Publishing."
    Poliester 2.6 (verano 1993): 18–27.

Mishima, Yukio. *Confessions of a Mask.* Trans. Meredith Weatherby. 1958. New York:
    New Directions, 1968.

———. *Forbidden Colors.* Trans. Alfred H. Marks. 1968. New York: Berkeley, 1974.

Morris, David B. *The Culture of Pain.* Berkeley: University of California Press, 1991.

Smith, Paul Julian. *Laws of Desire: Questions of Homosexuality in Spanish Writing and
    Film, 1960–1990.* Oxford: Oxford University Press, 1992.

Snyder, Robert Lance, ed. *Thomas De Quincey: Bicentenary Studies.* Norman: Univer-
    sity of Oklahoma Press, 1985.

Stoller, Robert J. *Pain and Passion: A Psychoanalyst Explores the World of S&M.* New
    York: Plenum, 1991.

Viegener, Matias. "Men Who Kill and the Boys Who Love Them." *Critical Quarterly*
    36.1 (spring 1994): 105–114.

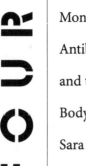

FOUR

Monobodies,

Antibodies,

and the

Body Politic:

Sara Levi Calderón's

Dos mujeres

Society is never a disembodied spectacle.
—John O'Neill, *Five Bodies*

In the current cultural climate of demolished walls and toppled public monuments, it seems noteworthy, even a bit disconcerting, to find in place an internationally orchestrated and promoted art exhibition such as "Mexico: Splendors of Thirty Centuries," which made the rounds of U.S. museums from New York to Los Angeles before it moved on to Monterrey, Mexico, in 1992. Through this officially sanctioned assemblage of diverse images clustered around the unifying concept of the alleged splendors of a "unitary will" (as Octavio Paz writes in the introductory essay for the exhibit catalogue [4]) stretching from the Mesoamerican past to the 1990s, there is insinuated a narrative continuum, a totalizing story of unbroken Mexican cultural threads woven across time and space, whose mythos represents the basis and overt legitimation of modern Mexico. This manifest proclamation—and, one might add, exportation—of identity is particularly revealing at the present time when the breaching of national boundaries, already a reality because geographical barriers are so porous where labor sources and mass media technoculture are concerned, has been sanctified by NAFTA, the free trade agreement negotiated between the governments of the United States, Mexico, and Canada. Such an agreement, in place since January 1994 in spite of popular protests such as those of Subcomandante Marcos and the peasants of the state of Chiapas, would appear to necessitate a reinforcement (or renegotiation) of what it means to be a real part of the Mexican nation. How this myth of national identity functions and (if indeed it continues to function) whether it is becoming, as Mexican anthropologist and cultural journalist Roger Bartra suggests, "dysfunctional" (12) are, at least in part, the subjects of this essay, whose main concerns are the complex relationships between individuals and communities. Such relationships are represented in a variety of literary texts produced by both established and new authors over the past few years. In particular, we might consider a character such as Valeria, from Levi Calderón's novel *Dos mujeres (The Two Mujeres)*, who is at once a child of Jewish refugees, a lesbian, a middle-aged woman in a country oriented toward youth, the (potential) inheritor of at least part of the family's fortune, and a student. Whether these characteristics can be made to coalesce into some coherent sense of identity or are merely fragments of the modern sense of self are issues central to this discussion. The violence of such a synthesis, and its required or implied sacrifices, may be the greatest antithesis to any sense of autonomy.

In spite of what critic Homi K. Bhabha accurately sees as the impossible unity of the nation as a permanent symbolic force, given the transitional nature of social realities and the imagined community's constant coming-into-being as a system of cultural signification, one nevertheless cannot deny the real and persistent attempts to create an official "aura" (Brennan 58) of national identity. This project is proposed through the invention of an evolutionary narrative of historical and social continuity and progress that includes as well "the narcissism of self-generation" (Bhabha 1) or zero degree of national identity. The project of nationalist discourse, then, is to excise any and all images of conflict or dissidence, and instead to celebrate the splendors of the formation of the one from the many, the composite one, thus "securing an identification between politics and culture . . . [and establishing] a structural relation between the nature of culture and the peculiarities of the state" (Bartra 10). The naturalizing of this holistic conception of national unity—a tacit agreement as to the origins, heroes, genealogies, and collective project of which, as ex-president Salinas has affirmed, "we [Mexicans] are *all* proud" (quoted in the exhibition program)—is grounded in the relative homogenization and coherence of political culture, in Mexico a legitimizing process hardly coherent with the economic development typical of the late twentieth century.[1] In this context, therefore, we must consider — as Jürgen Habermas strongly argues in his social analysis — the national project of modernity along with the process of modernization without viewing the former (the cultural) as either a necessary cause of or a precedent for the latter (the social) but rather viewing the two as pieces of the dynamic whole of everyday life. Modernization — "the capitalist transformation of a society, based on industry, science, and secular institutions . . . , the *real state* of capitalist social and economic development" — and modernity — "the imaginary [or imagined] country whose legitimating network traps civil society" — as defined by Bartra (15; emphasis added) are out of sync in Mexico except in the rhetoric of official culture. In other words, one might accurately conclude that Mexico's incomplete but institutionalized modernity (via the vehicle of the PRI, the Partido Revolucionario Institucional [Institutional Revolutionary Party]) is a modernity of excess — or an excess of modernity that masks the misery behind the splendors. Such "misery" takes many forms, most if not all experienced by those people on the margins of the more conspicuous "benefits" allocated to but a few. Just as the face of urban modernity hides the rural poverty and land disputes of long-suppressed indigenous inhabitants, it also employs the masquerade of tolerance to gloss over the possible real political dissidence of some members of society. In addition, modernity's disguising countenance puts a (harmless) political spin on dissent among certain individuals of the middle classes, for example, in order to push the problems of the lower classes into the background as inconveniences to be tolerated for the sake of the rest of the population. The cultural and economic freedoms of the middle classes are themselves posited on this very glossing over of heterogeneity in favor of "the imaginary" of modernity.

As Bartra writes, "the country is replete with modernity, but thirsty for modernization" (15). For the resolution of this discrepancy, he proposes the necessity of "la desmodernidad" (demodernization) (11), a term he relates in satirical fashion both to the existence of "un *desmadre* económico" (the mother of all economic disasters) and to the hope of that universal buzzword "postmodernity," which he defines as "the constant transgression of all borders . . . , [the possibility of being Mexican] without subjecting oneself to a state or territory: [the experience] of a deterritorialization and denationalization of the intellectuals" (15). In such a scenario, a "denationalization" in the geographical sense would seem to identify a process of "nationalizing" by signaling the specifically Mexican intellectual as a free-floating entity. There is, then, nationality without the nation. To put it another way, might one actually become more identifiably Mexican by traversing the borderlines put in the way for economic reasons in order to exercise the powers of cultural discourse? Is "exile" (immigration?) part and parcel of being Mexican?

One might ask whether in place of modernism's original concept of oppositionality, its "rebelling against all that is normative," (Habermas 5), there should be substituted an infinite plurality of shifting cultural artifacts and positions. Is some individual decentered or "deterritorialized" subject to be considered the only plausible basis for representation, since any mention of a collective project raises immediate fears of some type of master narrative of nationalism? We shall examine both the hopes and the realities represented by these concepts in terms of the Mexican cultural context and those who are drawn, willingly or otherwise, into participation. In the case of Levi Calderón's novel, we need also consider those characters who reject such integration and choose instead to leave the country. Yet the paradox of such "deterritorialization" is that it is indicative of the very privileges it seeks to deny. What appears to be resistance is, for all intents and purposes, collaboration or liberation (the freeing of the individual who does not attempt to respond in other ways to the exercise of the "law").

A conflation of "lo moderno" (modernity) and "lo extensivo" (quantity) is what Sara Sefchovich cites as the axis of official political culture in contemporary Mexico (261). She argues that in recent times the rule of thumb has been "more to consume" equals "a more modern nation." She summarizes that

> la cultura en México ha consistido, lo mismo que la economía, en acumulación, en dar más: más conferencias, más número de ejemplares en las ediciones de libros, más museos, conciertos, películas, casas de cultura, premios, festivales, homenajes y conmemoraciones. Cultura en México quiere decir . . . un Estado promotor que cuando no organiza directamente, entonces, patrocina o apoya, o por lo menos permite todos los eventos y publicaciones que deseen hacer los intelectuales, y que incluyen todas las posibilidades del quehacer de la mente y de las manos, siempre y cuando no se exceda el único límite que son las críticas dirigidas contra él y contra los mitos que nos alimentan. Hoy como nunca en nuestra historia y como en pocos países del mundo la oferta de posibilidades cultu-

rales en México excede cualquier fantasía, sueño o deseo. Quizá por esta
tradición histórica que le da tanto peso a la imitación, quizá por nuestro
viejo deseo de ser aceptados por el mundo como país civilizado, o quizá
por nuestros persistentes afanes de modernidad. (262)
[Culture in Mexico has consisted of accumulation, the same as in the
economy; it has meant producing more: more conferences, more publication runs of books, more museums, concerts, films, cultural centers,
prizes, festivals, homages, and tributes. Culture in Mexico means . . . a
promotional State that even when it does not directly organize, then it
either sponsors or supports, or at the very least permits all of the events
and publications that intellectuals might wish to have, including all of the
mental and physical possibilities imaginable, as long as one boundary is
not overstepped—there cannot be any criticism directed against the State
itself or against any of the myths that nourish it (us). Today as never before in our history and as in few other countries in the world, the supply
of cultural possibilities in Mexico exceeds any fantasy, dream, or human
desire. Perhaps this comes from our historical tradition that has given so
much importance to imitation, perhaps it comes from our long-standing
desire to be accepted by the rest of the world as a civilized country, or
perhaps we owe it all to our anxious pursuit of modernity.]

These splendors of modernity are signaled by the ability to offer consumers
what they as a nation, as Mexicans, want (or at least what they think they
want, or are told they want). This boils down to an endless accumulation of
products paralleled by an equally vast series of symbolic goods of diverse and
even contradictory nature, all made available through privatized companies
and enterprises that front for the state, wrested from their original contexts
and assembled into a collection that can be "brokered" (see Hollander 47) as
the images establishing Mexico's place in the New World Order just as works
of art are traded at auction. Rather than decentering Mexican culture (after
Bartra), this self-promotion identifies it as a strategic clearinghouse for things
flowing north as well as south over its borders. In this sense, the image of modern Mexico is one of middleman par excellence, an icon of tolerance allowing
anything and everything into its cultural horizons with no suggestion of dis-
crimination or persecution, but rather, as every Mexican presidential candidate in recent memory has stressed, "transparencia." Loosely translated, this

term means a process that is transparent (hides nothing), clean, irreproachable, untainted by fraud, open, and "democratic." It would thus at least sound
as if everyone and every aspect of society could participate in a free and open
dialogue.

The discourse of this so-called transition to democracy and modernity has
been overseen by a trinity of "presiding 'angels' " (Goldman 23): U.S.-educated
economist Carlos Salinas de Gortari, poet and Nobel Prize-winner Octavio
Paz, and Emilio Azcárraga, Jr., the majority shareholder of the international
media conglomerate Televisa. Together they have carefully edited and packaged an image of Mexico as a unique "work of art" (the phrase is taken from a
paid advertisement that appeared in *New York Times* in the fall of 1990) worthy
of a place in any discriminating connoisseur's collection. In what can only be
termed a masquerade of modernity, the state's official guarantee of personal
integrity and individual rights is relentlessly emphasized as the cornerstone of
this new nation. Once again, however, the mask is composed only of the rhetoric covering the actual reality behind what has been called "el eje de un trato
[social] civilizado y *moderno*" (the core of a civilized *modern* [social] order)
(González Rodríguez xi; emphasis added). At the same time the contradiction
continues in the overt celebration of "what is truly modern in modernity, the
tolerance for radical change, novelty, the unusual [while still finding oneself
in actuality] vilified, or worse, ignored, (or worse still, embraced, lionized) by
the public representatives of bourgeois modernity" (Pippin 41). The key concept here is that of public spectacle, of embracing critique and democratic
pluralism while simultaneously legislating against "dissidence" or resistance.
Such official acts have taken the form of strict new legislation, for example,
against the broad category of "delitos sexuales" (sexual crimes) and pornography, censoring what is deemed obscene or "sucio, feo, intolerable" (dirty,
ugly, intolerable) (González Rodríguez x), whatever this might or might not
encompass. A second step has been to disarm alternative ideas, projects, and
individuals by means of an apparent tolerance and even some forms of benign
promotion. Once again, the latter suggests Sefchovich's assessment of "dar
más" (greater quantity), the ideology that more is better because a multiplicity
of discourses can coexist in a harmless narrative soup, the result of a liberal act
of public generosity toward "all Mexicans" (to paraphrase Salinas's earlier pro-
nouncement). Both actions—censorship and tolerance—are proclaimed to be
the willing sacrifice, "[el] costo de las modernizaciones" (the price to be paid

for modernization) (González Rodríguez xi), in order to maintain the physical and moral health of the national agenda. Paz finds the ultimate symbol of such individual freedom in the free market, the last bastion to be conquered by "modernity" (Fazio 184) and the perfect venue for the practice of pluralism and tolerance. The cultural artifacts of this free market include, of course, products and images of all kinds, among them books and works of art.

Within the Mexican political economy of modernization, the legitimated existence of plural society is to be balanced in some fashion between a liberal spirit of acceptance or tolerance and "un ejercicio moderno de la autoridad, porque, sin menoscabo de la participación y el acuerdo, no renuncia [el estado] a sus responsabilidades de hacer prevalecer el interés general" (a modern exercise of authority, because, without diminishing participatory politics and reaching an accord, [the state] does not waive its responsibility to have the general interest prevail) (Salinas). This is communicated through the images of an erotic economy as well. The lived physical bodies that constitute the larger body politic, what philosopher John O'Neill vividly calls "the very flesh of society" (1985, 22–23), are the terrain in which all social behavior is grounded and all political life is rooted. The circulation of these images is based, according to O'Neill's schema, on a three-level interrelated model of the body politic. The model is composed of the bio-body (the domain of the family, the discourse of well-being and health), the productive body (the discourse of self-control, production, work, and surplus), and the libidinal body (the realm of the personal, happiness, creativity, contentment, desire, fantasy). While Salinas constantly has made reference in his public addresses to a horizon of progress for the individual and the family, suggesting not just an administrative power over lived bodies but also the continued production of other (similar if not duplicate) bodies restrained within the parameters required by the agenda of modernization, there exists also a concurrent discourse of "civic privatism" and "public depoliticization" (O'Neill 1985, 77). Fostered by the state, on the one hand this encourages the pursuit of consumption and leisure and, on the other, it promotes a "therapeutic" (O'Neill 1985, 138–139) model of a society whose health and well-being are guaranteed by a celebration of the splendors of youth, fitness, beauty, affluence, and heterosexuality (reproduction). These are the very qualities needed, the nation is told, for the smooth functioning of modernization; this is the perfect prescription for a healthy body politic.

To put this another way, plurality is fine if on the surface everyone looks and buys the same, i.e., as "identical consumers of identical goods" (Van Den Abeele xii). And it is also true that "consumers can be taught to disvalue their biological bodies entirely, except as those bodies are reappraised in the willing consumption of industrially mediated experience" (O'Neill 1985, 101); in this sense the physical (biological) body is placed at the service of productivity and reproductivity, with individual and family "health" defined as necessary aspects of the smooth functioning of the societal machine. Such a proposition is once again justified by its linkage to the benefits for the underlying identity of the nation. Moreover, the therapeutic authorities of advertising, the culture industry, and the media including film, television, radio, and videos intervene in the life of those outside the agency of the family to cure (no longer to discipline or punish—after all, this is the allegedly modern, post-1968 state) any individual who refuses to render service to the forces of production alone. Those so-called aberrant members of society, who reject becoming "mono-bodies" (O'Neill 1989, 81) bound to the workplace as the widely touted locus of free exchange and theoretically equal subjects under the social contract, are judged to contaminate the health and well-being of the nation. The regulated body, then, the one whose health depends on self-control and desires channeled into the streamlined production and consumption of an egalitarian, classless, and participatory "modern" Mexico (according to official rhetoric at least), is the product of the studied indifference and tolerance so glorified by and assimilated into the official culture of the metropolis. For if it is true, as Carlos Monsiváis asserts, that the population explosion of the cities has led to the cultivation of a "deliberate ignorance" (72) of others and an avowed disinterest in the overt censorship of any behavior, it is equally true that the media promotion of an international culture of infinite options has paved the way for what Sefchovich has already called the aspirations of "lo extensivo" or the goal of accumulation as the principal and incontrovertible sign of societal modernization and the clearest form of the already mentioned civic privatism and public depoliticization. Owing to the sheer quantity of citizens flocking to the city in search of opportunity and fortune, this moment signals the transition to a culture that ceremoniously looks the other way when it comes to dissidence. No one is overtly censured as long as they have the economic means to be an exemplary consumer. (When they have no such means, tolerance disappears.) It must be noted that Monsiváis equates modernity with Americanization (71) and that he calls the consumption of the flood of transnational media images an act of "cultural voyeurism" (73) that stimulates a desire for imitation, a definite "reappraisal" of the biological body by technological mediation (see O'Neill 1985, 101). This process is subsequently funneled into the discourse on national identity, and so a circular cultural movement ensues.

Inoculating the body politic against alternative political and cultural agendas, the official discourse of modernization allows the free circulation of a novel like *Dos mujeres* (1990) by Sara Levi Calderón, for instance. Although its contents could conceivably represent a serious challenge to the unitary concept of community based on ethnic origin and shared history (both of the main characters are descendants of Jewish immigrants who came to Latin America to escape the persecution of the Holocaust), class (one character is wealthy and one is a struggling artist, a fact both find it hard to overcome throughout the text), and sexual preference (Valeria and Genovesa both come out as lesbians in the course of the novel), the novel's best-seller status would seem to contradict its potential "danger" for society.[2] The ambiguities contained in the very concept of tolerance are evident in the pages of the narrative, and the numerous scenes of violence contained therein (between father and daughter, brother and sister, mother and sons) rend once and for all the superficial image of national harmony.

As the book cover of the Spanish edition puts it, this is "Una historia fuera de lo común, un amor que enfrenta un antagonismo con la sociedad y se expresa de una y mil formas. Una novela erótica que profundiza en la relación de dos mujeres que se aman sobre todas las cosas" (An uncommon story of a love that confronts social antagonism and expresses itself in a thousand and one ways. An erotic novel that delves into the relationship between two women who above and beyond everything else are in love with each other). The fact that it *is* a love story, complete with a happy ending and a utopian escape (exile?) to an island paradise, masks much of the possible challenge to social structures, however. In any event, an allowance for variety seems to be made here, because market exposure to the stories of these members of the political and cultural community, two Jewish women in Mexico City, is used in this context to stave off any real threats to so-called orderly conduct. The atmosphere of peace and prosperity that Salinas has proclaimed all Mexicans enjoy remains untouched, preserved intact by means of a liberal discourse of moral immunization. If the human body is potentially both the flesh of society *and* the text of protest, then social consensus is actually maintained and not ruptured by the allowance of a small dose—a novel here and there, the Semana Cultural Gay (Gay Culture Week) at the Universidad Nacional Autónoma de México, roundtables, films, plays, and a certain number of periodicals—into circulation in the body politic to build up a capacity of resistance and to counteract subsequent (pathogenic) attack by collective organisms. Singular events, individual narratives, and carefully controlled scenarios build up an immunity in the body politic; the only dangers that remain are collective organizations and the formation of possible communities. (But this is far from Levi Calderón's story.) We must take note that the operative word here is *collective:* the organization of alternatives to the official version of the nation joins individuals in movements with agendas for radical change. Identity politics, on the other hand, can be judged as the manageable isolation of alleged invaders in an otherwise harmoniously functioning group of social organs. The book's characters, Genovesa and Valeria, are but two individuals living against the current.

But although Monsiváis, for example, cites October 2, 1978, as the precise date for the beginning of so-called tolerance toward homosexuals in Mexico, the basis of that ostensibly democratic public acceptance has been greatly eroded since. On that tenth anniversary of the Tlatelolco massacre, a large contingent of gay men and women joined the commemorative march through the streets of Mexico City, showing open solidarity and shared militancy with sectors of the political left. It would appear that the social agendas of the left and of the gay community coincided, at least for a time, as José Rafael Calva has the character Carlos reveal in *Utopía gay.* This was not to last, however, for the emphasis on class and economic issues would return to split the two factions into opposing camps. Starting in the late 1970s, a drive by President López Portillo to foster a visible climate of democracy actively sought the participation of more political groups in the electoral process (a move that appeared to encourage pluralism but in reality solidified the official institutions of the PRI, as witnessed even as recently as the presidential elections of 1994). The ensuing honeymoon between political groups and government agencies was cut short by the "crisis" of the 1980s. The retrenchment of social classes in Mexico after the oil boom fizzled in 1982 produced a critical situation within the nascent gay and lesbian movements, which had aligned themselves with the human rights agenda of the left. This process of realignment began to drive a wedge between the social and economic classes that was to culminate in the formation of what many have referred to as the *nuevo porfiriato* (second coming of

Porfirio Díaz's dictatorship) of the past decades. Under this cultural and economic structure, the concept of tolerance is relegated to the more educated
and affluent circles of the nation — those in control of the media, the economy,
and investment in the arts — or, as Juan Carlos Bautista observes, "la tolerancia
[es] para quien pudiera pagarla" (tolerance belongs to those who can afford
it) (60). These indeed appear to be parts of the splendorous vision those who
would don the mask of modernity have of certain individual rights in Mexican society, accompanied by the hope that the same vision might some day
trickle down to those in more misery and less splendor. Bautista goes so far as
to lament the loss of oppositionality in this process of fragmentation ("public
depoliticization"), not by proposing a glorification of the permanently periph-
eral, but in terms of "la pérdida de los beneficios de la marginalidad a cambio
de las dudosas ventajas de la tolerancia del consumo" (the loss of the benefits of marginality in exchange for the doubtful advantages of the tolerance
of consumer society) (60). An identity based on the acquisition and hoarding
of consumer goods and on the values of the marketplace puts an end to solidarity and a sense of community while it accentuates class differences (who
can join the buying frenzy and to what extent). This is just an alternate way of
pointing to the economic differences created between those with first access to
modernization and those still "thirsty" for it (as Bartra has written [15]).

While two recent best-sellers,[3] Angeles Mastretta's *Arráncame la vida* (1985)
(*Mexican Bolero*, 1989) and Laura Esquivel's *Como agua para chocolate* (1989)
(*Like Water for Chocolate*, 1992) celebrate the heterosexual female subject
coming of age in a unitary counterpoint with national music (the bolero) and
typical national recipes (the novel's subtitle is "Novela de entregas mensuales
con recetas, amores y remedios caseros" [A novel in monthly installments
with recipes, romances, and remedies]), respectively, the sexual economy of
Dos mujeres is decidedly dual. Within the text, the representation of the unified body/body politic is problematized by means of the *retrato hablado* (word
portrait) (263) — a concept reminiscent of Gertrude Stein's use of the same
phrase to reflect a bridge between visual and linguistic representations of identity — and by means of the examination of the still photographs produced by
"la máquina de congelar momentos" (the instrument that freezes moments)
(193) through which two complex social identities and a novel-within-a-novel
are constructed. Rather than the integrationist tone of the bildungsroman, in
which a narrating subject provides the reader with clues to the inner struggles

that accompany the process of unifying his or her experiences into *one* coherent voice, *Dos mujeres* maintains a sense of contradictory identities that coexist to the end. Moreover, not only is there a physical and emotional relationship between two women — Genovesa the artist and Valeria the writer — but each is presented as two women in one: "La que me permitía gozar plenamente de la vida y la otra que me lo impedía" (The one who lets me fully enjoy life and the other one who keeps me from doing so) (30). These double narratives address all three levels of the body politic (according to O'Neill's schema), as well as the tension of their intersections, in the social articulation of each of the subjects. How the biological body (in the form of the family), the productive body (the realm of work), and the libidinal body (desire and fantasy) are experienced by the characters Genovesa and Valeria forms the core of this narrative. The patriarchal European family, the writer and artist, and the desire of two women for each other are the particularities of the story. What becomes most problematic, however, and the element that might potentially tie this narrative to a discourse of practicable contestatory modernism, is the question of the agency of these subjects within a collectivity and of the concepts of resistance around which an alternative community, if any, might cohere.[4] In other words, is *Dos mujeres* proposing a discourse of alterity, a program of radical otherness even in the midst of social compulsion, or does it represent a relatively more comfortable integration? To what is this integration owed? Do the characters stand apart on their own or is there a feeling of shared community with others? And where does the artist/writer find her "home"?

Instead of a public exhibition framed in the space of an art gallery or museum, *Dos mujeres* offers the reader splendors of a different sort, ones kept in an album of the family's history — "mi herencia visual" (my visual legacy) (15) as Valeria calls it — which reveals and solidifies the topographies of these women's desires and their "lived bodies." Even before the two women's time together begins, Valeria finds herself at a crossroads in her life regarding family, education, career, and marriage, and tries to sort out her choices by scouring the photo album and scrutinizing the portraits of her female predecessors. She rejects them one by one as removed from her own feelings, or as intractably critical of her. When she inadvertently spills a drink on one photograph, Valeria tries only halfheartedly to save it from imminent erasure. As subjects frequently, almost incessantly, held hostage by familial and corporate institutions, Valeria and Genovesa are presented with opportunities to confront those very centers of power and thereby to politicize the realm of everyday life out of tolerance into critique. Such an encounter between individual and social forces might not resolve the complex situation once and for all, but it could point the way to a radical split. Yet both Genovesa and Valeria seem to avoid these confrontations, preferring instead to flee. The irony of this "solution" is its eerie reminder of the exile that brought their families to Mexico in the first place.

It matters little whether or not there is film in the camera when Genovesa and Valeria are together, however. Their lived experiences are captured in and on their very flesh, and when each is found studying herself in the mirror—after their first meeting, after running away to San Francisco, during their stolen hours in Cuernavaca over All Souls' weekend—this act seems to fix an image of the moment almost as if the click of a camera were actually being heard. Freezing instants and identities in time, the camera documenting their experiences (the eye of the narrating *I*) forces the observer to respond to the objects and individuals of this world in a conscious way rather than through mandated acceptance or tolerance. The lens focuses in on their surroundings in a one-on-one encounter. For the two women, "La cara escondida de Nueva York" (New York's hidden [cruel] face) (95) is the one they choose to seek out, not the city's glossy tourist mask. The details of Avenue A, heroin addicts, and ghetto life are registered in their filmless snapshots as vividly as the details of Genovesa's face and body are fixed in the eye and lingered over in the mind's eye of Valeria. However, just as Roland Barthes's volume *Camera Lucida* traps Valeria's gaze in the bookstore window, and as reality lives beyond the aesthetically captured moment—"el beso que nos dimos duró más que el click" (our kiss lasted longer than the [camera's] click) (87)—in Barthes's words, "the Photograph always leads the corpus I need back to the body I see" (4). Theirs is a journey back to an encounter with a specific reality and corporality, not to a mere shadow of a lived desire but back to the very object of desire in the flesh. Instead of a displacement "fueled by the inaccessibility of the object and dissatisfaction with the real" (Hutcheon 144), a desire endlessly anticipatory and constantly deferred into the future, Valeria's desire is finally actualized in the present in multiple spaces and forms. "Mi deseo por ella era tan evidente que decidí no luchar contra él" (I felt such strong desire for her that I decided not to fight against it) (36), she observes as she searches for the language adequate to express what she feels. Valeria finds the words in a work of literature, of all places—as she confesses, "Tuve deseos de leerle el archileído capítulo siete de *Rayuela*" (I wanted to read her the thousand-times-read chapter seven in [Julio Cortázar's] *Hopscotch*) (57) — since she identifies something of Cortázar's *flâneuse* character La Maga in Genovesa's free spirit. The mere evocation of that brief first-person narration of the ardent encounter between the mouths and fingertips of two lovers — gender unspecified — is enough to arouse Valeria's passion even more, creating a corresponding effect in Genovesa and precipitating their own physical encounter. As in Cortázar's text, Genovesa is Valeria's creation even before they touch; the mint candy that precipitates their contact is just a catalyst of the fantasy already imagined. The beginning of chapter seven in *Rayuela* reads: "Toco tu boca, con un dedo toco el borde de tu boca, voy dibujándola como si saliera de mi mano . . . , y me basta cerrar los ojos para deshacerlo todo y recomenzar, hago nacer cada vez la boca que deseo" (I touch your mouth, with one finger I touch the edge of your mouth, I outline its shape as if it came out of my hand . . . , and it's enough for me to close my eyes to erase it all and start over, the mouth I desire is reborn each time I begin again) (48). The same holds true for the two women in this novel, and their only reminder of the society "outside" comes with the ringing of the telephone that interrupts the ceremony. Such intrusions are frequently the only vestigial reminders of a "real" world from which they have chosen to flee in order to create their own safe haven.

   The center of contact between Valeria and Genovesa is their visual perception, each acting as a mirror for the other's actions and relentlessly observing the other to possess her — and thereby to find a sense of self — by means of this reciprocal gaze. Valeria concludes that to part the veil covering Genovesa's innermost secrets she must begin with her eyes: "pronto supe que la entrega de su cuerpo era lenta. Había que acariciarla con la mirada" (I soon found out that she gave herself slowly. You had to caress her with your eyes) (60). It is through this look that Valeria identifies her own desire, which in turn becomes Genovesa's in a process of identification and appropriation. "Tenemos la mirada idéntica" (Our eyes look exactly the same) (76), Genovesa confesses in alarm during one of their first encounters after a series of failed attempts at intimacy. Her first reaction is to cover up her eyes, but she subsequently accepts the feelings brought on by this "contagious" (65) desire. Ubiquitous mirrors add to the series of narcissistic images, reflecting back the bodies of the two women so that they might identify themselves as the real subjects of this passion. The mirror becomes a medium, an "accomplice" (71) that fixes and multiplies the corporal presence of Genovesa and Valeria much as the eye of the camera does for the spectator. Yet both the mechanical and technical means of reproducing the image, in Barthes's words once again, reinforce the need to revert back to the material body from which the representation is drawn. And it is in this very "materiality" where many of the paradoxes of the narrative occur, as we shall see shortly.

Their erotic moments, far from the sedate portraits and posed self-portraits of the formal art exhibit, are declarations of pleasure unhinged, in a sense, from the framework of fixed representations of gender that circulate in an essentially patriarchal and heterosexual economy. They embody, in fact, what Barthes refers to as the "ecstasy" of the photograph, a confrontation with "the wakening of intractable reality," rather than a subjection to "the civilized code of perfect illusions" (119) of reality-turned-art. Backing off somewhat (though never completely) from consumer society's norms of desire—O'Neill's concept of the experiences of the biological body mediated by technology—and perhaps even its pandering to the libidinal body as a mechanism of control, a body brought into compliance by "titillating and ravishing its sensibilities while at the same time it standardizes and packages libidinal responses to its products" (O'Neill 1985, 81), *Dos mujeres* is not beyond culture and politics but squarely within their very spaces. Even as Valeria and Genovesa close themselves off from the geography of the "outside" in their villas and hotels, carousels and restaurants, spas and exotic hideaways, they cannot escape the residual effects of what surrounds them and what they have assimilated. Their proposition to carve out alternative spaces for themselves, whether inside or outside Mexico, seems to rely almost absolutely on the financial support of those most critical of their relationship. Even an all-expenses-paid exile to New York or California does not remove the ultimate source of this so-called benefit: the wealth of Valeria's father. Despite any attempts at erasure, Valeria and Genovesa are drawn back from self-exile (and economic banishment) at least temporarily into the "belly of the beast," as it were, when a Mexican publishing company offers Valeria a contract for her autobiographical novel, endowing it with a symbolic capital absent from their "lived bodies." They reap the benefits of an artifact that circulates and stands in—unobtrusively—for their real lived bodies and actual presence. The narrative version of their shared life is a salable product because of its aesthetic (technological?) processing of the raw data of biological bodies having no such positive "value" on their own.

The object—*Dos mujeres*—assumes a material life in a society that offers no real space for its protagonists to inhabit. Thus, exile becomes their "vanishing point"—the "punto de fuga donde convergían todos los ángulos" (vanishing point where all angles meet) (37)—a position startlingly reminiscent of Bartra's proposal of a postmodern "deterritorialization" and "denationalization," discussed earlier. By disappearing across the border, *or* by disappearing within their own homeland, the two women fit the schema of national identity by being absorbed into the zone of tolerance, the true "vanishing point" for any Mexican lesbian couple. Only the representation, the story, remains.

Levi Calderón's text is suffused with a strong sense of the media and its gendered images, as indicated by the characters' encounters with the chic young inhabitants of the liberal tourist area of Mexico City, the Zona Rosa, in which tolerance is the official policy. Yet as they wander among these minor cosmopolitan deities, cloaked in designer splendor and the latest hairstyles amid "the debris of urban crime and desolation" (O'Neill 1989, 81) that constantly threaten to encroach on the artificial borders of this protected space, Genovesa and Valeria are still subjected to insults and threats. As they stroll arm in arm, aware of their refusal to be complicit in the masquerade of homogeneity, their consciousness of role playing is enhanced. From the very outset there is a sense of the need for acting and representation, for a simulacrum of life projected from behind a "disfraz de cada día" (an everyday disguise) (42). This begins with the Cavafy epigraph taken from "El Rey Demetrio" (King Demetrius), who, abandoned by the Macedonians in favor of another king, removed his visible symbols of power and took on another identity—as a commoner. The next scene of masquerade is Valeria's account of her coming-of-age fifteenth birthday party, followed by her wedding, whose paralyzed gestures and tableaux she recounts in the third person as if they belonged to someone outside herself, and concluding with her violent and unresolved dealings with her family. Seeking a liberation from this immersion in the common "we" promoted through cinematic and other mass media images of young, docile, heterosexual women, Valeria is seduced, both literally and figuratively, by the apparent freedom of the struggling young artist Genovesa, in whom she sees remnants of herself from earlier times. Fourteen years her junior, in denial of her own feelings for another woman and yet living the capitalist fantasy of the free market in which "amar a una mujer era una etapa por la que tenía que pasar" (loving a woman was only a stage she had to go through) (90) in order to be liberated and "modern," Genovesa is the catalytic figure that stimulates Valeria to project her fantasies outward and act upon them. Yet Genovesa's own reticence to commit to their relationship is a central part of the narrative.

At first, the very fantasy images culled from Hollywood films that Valeria has constantly criticized as part of her mother's upwardly mobile integrationist discourse are those she herself relies on for her own love story. Both her life and her narration of it are filled with descriptions taken from the movies: she sees women in terms of the movie stars promoted in these mass fantasies. Populated with internalized ideals of feminine beauty and eternal youth presented as somehow "natural" objects of desire, such as Mexico's legendary love balladeer Agustín Lara's vision of the equally legendary Mexican actress María Félix "bajo palmeras borrachas de sol" (under palm trees intoxicated by the sun) (84), they seem to be strangely compatible with her passion for Genovesa. This is true even though Valeria comments that her new twist on the classic love story does appear to break the stereotype of the implied actors for each role: "que fuera [la estrella de mi gran historia de amor] una mujer no era cualquier cosa" (that [my great love story] starred a woman was no minor thing) (61), she admits to herself. Her sense of a paradigmatic love story just waiting for the right individual to come along and play the role of the object of Valeria's grand passion (just as María Félix finds on the silver screen) eventually is overridden by the demand on her to construct an identity inside the domain of social reality rather than from a distant utopian space. From the carousel horses moving to the rhythms of singer Patti Smith's album "Horses," Valeria must move "outside" to the realm of social reality. The story is played out by its participants; it does not, and cannot, come prefabricated, like a one-size-fits-all garment to be stepped into. It is, instead, a process fraught with constant challenges by the biological and productive aspects of the body politic, which try to draw the women back into the traditional heterosexual family and productive/reproductive work structures.

"Yo me dejé llevar por ella" (I let myself be led by her) (10), Valeria concludes in retrospect, as if Genovesa were the personification, the absolute embodiment, of the other woman within herself who needs to be set free. Naively seen as a complete rupture with the past, this process cannot so easily banish into oblivion all social and cultural traces by mere wishful thinking. The break is presented as an apocalyptic moment: "lo anterior moría y el presente nacía golpeando" (the present moment was born with a bang and all that existed be-

fore died irrevocably away) (42); although later we are told that the split is not
so definitive. All of the "formaciones graníticas" (hard edges) (60) and "valores
introyectados" (internalized fears) (78) do not just fade away; they loom on the
horizon, ready to impede their passion and often able to do so, as in the moment Genovesa leaves for France at the end of the first part of the text. The second part of the book, ostensibly composed during the period when Genovesa
has returned to Europe to look after her drug-addicted cousin, chronicles the
skirmishes between Valeria and the law of the father.[5] Starting with her childhood, she narrates the regimentation of home, private school, synagogue, and
even her limited attempts at a social life. The two pillars of control are her
father and her brother Efraín, the only son and source of greatest pride for the
family. Between them, both before and after she meets Genovesa, they share
the task of keeping Valeria "decent" in the eyes of the neighbors, the Jewish
community, and the rest of their social class. In the chapter entitled "La gol-
piza" (The beating), for instance, she recounts the physical violence of a leather
belt used by her father to instill on her flesh the traditional "values" she innocently flouts in the exploration of her adolescent sexuality with her friend and
schoolmate Pier in the secrecy of the school's bathrooms. On this occasion,
despite the fact that she is narrating an episode from the past many years after
its actual occurrence and despite her declared desire to wipe the slate clean and
begin all over again ("all that existed before died irrevocably away"), this section ends with her total enervation. Left alone in her room to suffer the pain
of the lashes and "learn her lesson" not to embarrass her family, Valeria tries
to feel pleasure in her body once again but finds she is unable to recover such
delightful sensations. Both pain and pleasure leave her body: "no sentía nada"
(I felt nothing) (126). She must learn to overcome the marks of the "law," and
this takes the amount of time represented by the remainder of the text.

Even though Efraín was the one who consciously precipitated this violence
by telling their parents what boys were saying in the schoolyard about her,
and her father was the one who executed the punishment in the name of the
family's honor, Valeria casts the blame for the entire episode on her mother.
Instead of being her daughter's ally, she took the side of the law. Valeria remembers, "Nunca iba a perdonarle que hubiera permitido que mi papá me
golpeara tan brutalmente y, peor aún, que dijera que mi hermano sólo quería
mi bien" (I would never forgive her for letting my father beat me so cruelly
and, on top of that, saying that my brother had only wanted what was best for

me) (130). The two male figures of authority have usurped the voices of the women, which might have otherwise expressed defense of or support for one another. This leaves Valeria cast out into solitude. This is what she is thinking on Yom Kippur, the Jewish Day of Atonement and forgiving, when all of the women in the synagogue are removed from the gallery for making too much noise and disturbing the worship of the men. Not only does she have to sit in the company of the woman who, at least in theory if not in practice, could have comprehended her anguish and interceded for her in the face of patriarchal justice, but they are silenced and banished as a group to a space outside the temple besides. As Valeria interrupted the course of her father's "life of honor" earlier, she now is too audible when religious practices and protocol call for her silence and submission to the "law."

As if this were not enough for her to recall, Valeria's mother places in her daughter's mind the threat that if she ever does anything "wrong" again it will kill her father and she will have to live with the consequences ever after. Corporal punishment left its mark on her for a long time, but this psychological control lasts even longer. After she has decided to stay with Genovesa and accept the idea that access to the family's money has been cut off, she agrees to meet her father for lunch and is told by him "Debes regresar a tus obligaciones [familiares] o, de lo contrario, vas a arrepentirte" (You must go back to your [family] duties. . . . otherwise, you'll regret it) (225). The form of this "regret" is never spelled out, but it need not be. It is enough for him to raise the threat of some retribution for her "sins." Shortly after their meeting, Valeria is notified that her father has suffered a heart attack and is in the hospital. His revenge is double: not telling her of his condition (she finds out from a distant relative that he is hospitalized) and concentrating his attention on her sons, ignoring her presence at his bedside. When she concludes that, in their harsh judgments against her, "Ellos eran la continuidad de mi padre" (They were just the same as my father) (233), as well as his implicit and complicit agents in the ransacking of her studio shortly before, she decides two things. Upon Genovesa's return and their reunion, Valeria and she make the choice to stay together—and to leave Mexico for Greece. But even wishful thinking will not erase these formative chapters of Valeria's life from intruding periodically on her thoughts and actions. The "formaciones graníticas" or monoliths of past experience are only worn down, a bit at a time; they do not disappear.

We must keep in mind here O'Neill's discussion of the therapeutic strategies of the state, with its proposal to cure transgressions against and within the integrity of the collective organism by cataloguing and predicting anti-social conduct (see O'Neill 1985, 139). In a sense, tolerance is the state's tactic against anticipated dissidence; it is a warning sign of a coming "danger" to be avoided. Alterity and resistance are thereby defused through their incorporation into a false space within the liberal community (the book is there, the women are not). This institutionalizes and celebrates a commitment by the individual to his or her own material desires and self-worth alone, and multiplies the agencies of the avowedly benign face of the (modern) state, which affords treatment and therapy to protect and serve the "distraught family" (O'Neill 1985, 145). From the discipline-and-punish model of Valeria's mother, father, brother, and sons, all of whom believe she can be beaten into correction, she passes to her husband Luis's curative care. After finding her in the shower with Sandra, another "liberated woman" and the wife of a close friend, Luis reaches the conclusion that his wife has simply not been taught the right lessons. She can be "cured" if he just tolerates her temporary transgression (of a personal nature, as he sees it, against himself alone). As Valeria recalls, he concludes that "[yo] no había aprendido a ser mujer" (the essential thing was that I hadn't learned to be a woman) (153), and Luis generously assures her that he will correct her erroneous course, as befits his position of power in the family and in the social structure. She recounts their discussion in terms of his condescending attitude toward her and his immediate assumption of control over the "situation": "Me comunicó acariciándome la cabeza que lo que yo tenía era una enfermedad y agregó que las enfermedades se curan. El iba a ayudarme" (Patting my head, he announced that what I had was an illness and illnesses can be cured. He was going to help me) (166). Instead of awaiting his proposed "treatment," she leaves home, tries to live in several different places including an ashram, and goes to acting classes. Putting to good use a bit of the antibody theory itself, she decides that by studying the art of the theater she can confront and counteract her own masquerade. By going through the violent public spectacle of breaking asunder the metaphorical "membrana violeta como un molusco que se ceñía a mi cuerpo" (violet membrane, like a mollusk, [that] enveloped my body) (167) since childhood, Valeria rejects the chic *Metropolitan* magazine version of heterosexual femininity surrounding and engulfing her. But she finds it much more difficult to abandon the class privileges accorded a woman of her social and economic background as the daughter of a wealthy Jewish (European) immigrant. Poverty becomes the hardest punishment for her to bear. Her liberty concerning sexual desires is so postulated on material comforts that, without her family as the fountain of financial support, even in rebellion, she is lost. She doesn't know "who she is." When her American Express card is rejected and she and Genovesa are stranded penniless on the California coast, after careful consideration Valeria arrives at the conclusion she has feared all along: "Ya me chingaron. Até cabos: ya me desheredaron" (They've screwed me. I put one and one together: they've just taken my inheritance away) (215). Once left without her class identity, embodied in the green plastic of a credit card "with privilege" and status, Valeria begins to "detest" (217) the freedom she has been defending, at least in theory, up to now. She no longer has the corollary freedom of movement—the control over places to travel, the possibility of escape, access to anywhere at any time, the seclusion of protective environments—that has always been hers. She decides for self-exile—from her parents, from her sons, and from the so-called national values that seem to follow her everywhere—in order to write the very same coming-out autobiographical novel we are reading. She turns it all into written language on the blank page.

The introjection of such an essentializing notion of liberty, a concept presented here as intrinsically valuable in some absolute and abstract form, and perhaps at best only marginally instrumental in the construction of an alternative identity, is quite problematical. It seems to posit a defense not of contestation and radical change, but of splintering and breaking off. Genovesa and Valeria take off for Greece; their discontentment leads to a Mediterranean island far from "home" (at least in a geographic sense). To paraphrase Bautista's remarks on the accessibility of tolerance for the well-to-do, this freedom might be rendered by the expression "each woman for herself." And this economy allows for much the same free circulation of privileged individual subjects around and around the social bloodstream as it does of national treasures back and forth across airwaves, movie screens, and museum halls, with cultural images and objects collected, organized, and exhibited by some free-market *bricoleur*. The activity of this entrepreneur who scrounges up bits and pieces of former constructs and masterfully recombines them to produce new creations is based on the process of modernization, and is used to confirm (in a perfectly circular argument) the existence of that very same process as well. By circularity I refer to the use of the self-fulfilling notion that the exhibitionism (pun intended) permitted to plurality and modernity in the social body's cultural products both validates what is contained in official discourse and convinces the recipient (reader, observer, cultural voyeur) that this will lead to that discourse's stated goals besides. (In other words, if everyone is allowed to speak—Valeria publishes her novel, which is set out on display among the rest of the stories being told—this confirms the true sign of a modern consumer culture.) We must ask ourselves, therefore, whether the deliberate ignorance of the inhabitants of the modern metropolis as observed by Monsiváis has the effect of offering self-sufficient subjectivity to replace the abandonment of any critical attempt to identify, on the one hand, communities of human experience. And whether on the other hand, those who use the production of a continuous supply of cultural goods that seem to offer an unbroken horizon (Rowe and Schelling 1) to control the official agenda in ever more insidious ways behind the mask of democracy in fact count on societal disorganization and a fear and loathing of narratives of mastery (Owens 65) as a strategy to demonize opposition. In the simplest terms, we might ask whether Levi Calderón's narrator is permitted to speak of her desire for another woman because, after all, this is the story of *only* two women. They are not indicative of the many, but merely *two* lone individuals who occupy a space of sanctioned— somehow legalized—opposition and who have the right to a certain amount of indulgence or tolerance because, in Valeria's words, "las mujeres de mi clase social podemos hacer de todo, siempre y cuando no sea en serio" (women in my social position were allowed to do anything as long as we didn't take it seriously) (206). The question remains as well regarding the "serious" reaction of the marketplace/society to the narrative contained in *Dos mujeres.*

In the schema of modernity, then, this text must be negotiated by the critical reader not only as a highly visible sign of Mexican "progress" in the arena of social tolerance, but as a marker of more complex societal relations as well. The "splendors" of modernity can be merely surface phenomena, leaving untouched the core of daily life and its victims. Whether *Dos mujeres* is a signal of something to be "taken seriously" (as Valeria remarks) as far as the lived experiences of lesbians in Mexico are concerned (and *which* lesbians), whether it mirrors the freedom of the marketplace or the "stages" a nation need go through to belong to an international community of modern societies, or whether it is a forerunner of a real alterity, these are all issues intimately bound into the story of these two women—a story with a deceptively simple title.

Notes

1   Bartra points out that the myth of national identity is "popular" and "anticapital-
ist," two reasons (leading to a loss of function) for its contradiction of the economic
policies of capitalism (see 12). It is possible, however, to consider the popular as
another locus of imposition from above, in particular as a populist strategy used to
gain or maintain power by the state. In the problematical 1994 Mexican elections,
for instance, the recourse to campaign populism and dedication to political reform
(in addition to other factors, of course) cost one candidate his life in Tijuana (Luis
Donaldo Colosio) and formed a central part of the platform of the winner, Ernesto
Zedillo Ponce de León. The rhetoric of populism, of course, may (and often does)
have little to do with real politics or the implementation of actual programs.

2   I have found no analysis of the reasons for its sales in Mexico, in contrast to the
promotion of the book in the United States (especially among academics) by Aunt
Lute Press and the gay press in general. My own experience reveals a less than methodical sales approach by the Mexican bookstores. After spending quite a while
browsing through the recent publications in one of the large Librería de Cristal
branch stores, I began to sort through what I might be able to afford and what
would, regrettably, have to be left behind. A young (male) clerk walked up to my
stacks of books, picked up Levi Calderón's from the pile of purchases yet in doubt,
and told me I really must buy this novel because (with a smile) I would really enjoy
it. How could I interpret this gesture? Was it salesmanship or targeting a consumer
by gender, nationality, etc.? It worked; I bought the book. On the other hand, I
later learned that Levi Calderón's father had bought up all the copies he could find
so it would not appear on bookstore shelves. Obviously, he was unsuccessful.

3   Carlos Monsiváis sees a political culture of both the left and the right coming
together over these cultural artifacts that have triumphed on the list of current or
recent best-sellers. He writes: "lo reconozcan o no, y mucho más de lo que se ad-
mite, se va unificando la cultura pública de la derecha y de la izquierda: las mismas
películas, los mismos libros de moda (García Márquez, Paz, Kundera, Yourcenar,
el Thriller, Asimov, Mastretta, John le Carré), la misma música: Bach, Mozart,
Madonna, el bolero. Fuera de las lecturas indispensables, de religión en un caso,
de mantenimiento esforzado de los rescoldos utópicos en otro, la izquierda y la
derecha obedecen a los dictados de la internacionalización cultural a la medida de
las posibilidades" (whether they accept it or not, and much more than anyone admits, the public culture of the right and of the left are becoming more and more one
and the same: the same movies, the same fashionable books [by García Márquez,
Paz, Kundera, Yourcenar, thrillers, Asimov, Mastretta, John le Carré], the same
music: Bach, Mozart, Madonna, romantic ballads. Outside the indispensable read-

ings, on religion in one instance, the forced upholding of the dying embers of utopia in the other, the left and the right obey all the dictates of cultural internationalization insofar as possible) (Aranda Luna 44). The transnational marketplace has homogenized the cultural one. One merely has to look at the rapid translation of *Like Water for Chocolate* into English and its success in international box offices, or the popularity of *Danzón* (Ballroom Dancing), directed by María Novaro, to find two more examples of just such "best-seller" status that have responded to NAFTA's promotion of an "internationally" legible and comprehensible Mexicanness. The joining of forces by the left and the right in the reopening of the Salón México, a famous dance hall of the early decades of the twentieth century, is an offshoot of the popularity of *Danzón* as well. Perhaps the search for sexual liberation and a sense of identity on the part of the character played by María Rojo in this film (a single mother working for Teléfonos de México, the national telephone company in the throes of forced modernization and technological upgrading) is one of the factors uniting the political culture of Mexico. Her return "home" when her brief adventure is over confirms the temporary nature of her search and the persistence of tradition in the face of change. (The state and its interests can rest easy at the end of the film.)

4   Rosamaría Roffiel's 1989 novel *Amora* (the title is a feminized version of the Spanish term of endearment *amor*—an equivalent of the English "dear" or "love") offers several notions of female community in much more concrete terms than does Levi Calderón's novel. These include the GRAPAV (Grupo de Ayuda a Personas Violadas [Support Group for Rape Victims]) and the Movimiento de la Liberación de la Mujer (Women's Liberation Movement), as well as the fem cooperative and even other, less formalized, structures of cooperation and self-help for women. Roffiel's narrative has been much less successful in economic terms, either in Mexico or abroad, then Levi Calderón's. It remains to be translated into English.

5   For a discussion of Freud, Lacan, sublimation of desire, and the "law," see Jeffrey Weeks's preface to Hocquenghem, 23–47. Here he clarifies that "This is not necessarily [a reference] to a real male parent but rather the symbolic representation of all Fathers: the Father is the authority" (29). In the case of Valeria, her brother, father, husband, and sons all impose (or try to impose) the law of the Father on the woman (the Daughter, in a symbolic sense akin to the authoritarian representation of the Father). Schools, religious institutions, and the workplace all function in similar ways to maintain the familial relationship of hierarchy and authority over the woman, who never gets to play the role of an (independent) adult, but rather is always held responsible to someone other than herself.

Works Cited

Aranda Luna, Javier. "Entrevista con Carlos Monsiváis." *Vuelta* 174 (mayo 1991): 43–46.

Barthes, Roland. *Camera Lucida: Reflections on Photography.* Trans. Richard Howard. New York: Hill and Wang, 1981.

Bartra, Roger. "Mexican *Oficio:* the Miseries and Splendors of Culture." Trans. Coco Fusco. *Third Text* 14 (spring 1991): 7–15.

Bautista, Juan Carlos. "¿El fin de la democracia gay?" *Nexos* 139 (julio 1989): 60–61.

Bhabha, Homi K. "Introduction: Narrating the Nation." In *Nation and Narration.* Ed. Homi K. Bhabha. London: Routledge, 1990. 1–7.

Brennan, Timothy. "The National Longing for Form." In *Nation and Narration.* Ed. Homi K. Bhabha. London: Routledge, 1990. 44–70.

Cortázar, Julio. *Rayuela.* 1963. Buenos Aires: Sudamericana, 1970.

Esquivel, Laura. *Como agua para chocolate.* Mexico City: Planeta, 1989.

———. *Like Water for Chocolate (A Novel in Monthly Installments with Recipes, Romances, and Home Remedies).* Trans. Carol Christensen and Thomas Christensen. New York: Doubleday, 1992.

Fazio, Carlos. "El tío Octavio y el escribidor." *Nuevo Texto Crítico* 6 (2° semestre 1990): 183–189.

Goldman, Shifra M. "Metropolitan Splendors: The Buying and Selling of Mexico." *Third Text* 14 (spring 1991): 17–25.

González Rodríguez, Sergio. "Pornografía y censura." *Nexos* 152 (septiembre 1990): ix–xi.

Habermas, Jürgen. "Modernity—an Incomplete Project." In *The Anti-Aesthetic (Essays on Postmodern Culture).* Ed. Hal Foster. Seattle: Bay Press, 1983. 3–15.

Hocquenghem, Guy. *Homosexual Desire.* Trans. Daniella Dangoor. 1972. Durham: Duke University Press, 1993.

Hollander, Kurt. "Report from Mexico (I): Art of the '80s in Monterrey." *Art in America* October 1991: 46–53.

Hutcheon, Linda. *The Politics of Postmodernism.* London: Routledge, 1989.

Levi Calderón, Sara. *Dos mujeres.* Mexico City: Diana, 1990.

———. *The Two Mujeres.* Trans. Gina Kaufer. San Francisco: Aunt Lute Books, 1991.

Mastretta, Angeles. *Arráncame la vida.* Mexico City: Océano, 1985.

———. *Mexican Bolero.* Trans. Ann Wright. London: Viking, 1989.

Monsiváis, Carlos. "Paisaje de batalla entre condones." *Nexos* 139 (julio 1989): 71–74.

O'Neill, John. "AIDS as a Globalizing Panic." *Public 3: Carnal Knowledge Issue.* Toronto: Public Access Collective, 1989. 77–85.

———. *Five Bodies: The Human Shape of Modern Society.* Ithaca, N.Y.: Cornell University Press, 1985.

Owens, Craig. "The Discourse of Others: Feminists and Postmodernism." In *The Anti-Aesthetic: Essays on Postmodern Culture*. Ed. Hal Foster. Port Townsend, Wash.: Bay Press, 1983. 57–82.

Paz, Octavio. "Will for Form." Introduction to *Mexico: Splendors of Thirty Centuries*. New York: Metropolitan Museum of Art, 1990. 3–38.

Pippin, Robert. B. *Modernism as a Philosophical Problem*. Cambridge: Basil Blackwell, 1991.

Roffiel, Rosamaría. *Amora*. Mexico City: Planeta, 1989.

Rowe, William, and Vivian Schelling. *Memory and Modernity: Popular Culture in Latin America*. London: Verso, 1991.

Salinas de Gortari, Carlos. "El Plan Nacional de Desarrollo 1989–1994." *Nexos* 139 (julio 1989): n.p.

Sefchovich, Sara. *México: País de ideas, país de novelas: Una sociología de la literatura mexicana*. Mexico City: Grijalbo, 1987.

Van Den Abeele, Georges. Introduction. *Community at Loose Ends*. Ed. Miami Theory Collective. Minneapolis: University of Minnesota Press, 1991.

Just Another
Material Girl?
La hermana secreta
de Angélica María
and the Seduction
of the Popular

From the movies we learn precisely how to hold a champagne
flute, kiss a mistress, pull a trigger, turn a phrase. In
romantic or adventure films, these feats are perfectly executed
and beautifully lit. The movies spoil us for life; nothing ever
lives up to them.
—Edmund White, *Genet: A Biography*

In a passage about halfway through his 1985 novel *En jirones* (In shreds), Mexican writer Luis Zapata has the character Sebastián articulate his rejection of
a larger-than-life vision of history, of "[los] sucesos grandilocuentes, operís-
ticos" (the grandiloquent, operatic events) (111–112) that make up what he
calls the cinematic version of his life. The representation of such a sequence
of events, he claims, covers up underlying tensions with a veil of social legiti-
macy. This judgment is followed immediately by a fervent expression of the
need to find a language in which to narrate instead "la petite histoire" (an
individual's story; microhistory, or what Spanish philosopher Miguel de Unamuno would term "intrahistoria," or inner history),[1] the intimate story of a
real passion lived by an individual as opposed to the extravagant and impassioned epic scenarios of official national history that subsume solitary voices
and their everyday reality. In other words, the language used to cloak narra-

tives and the garments draped over the topographies of human bodies must be rent in order to display what is covered up or what doesn't "fit in."

A young man physically and psychologically tortured by his on-again, off-again male lover—whose identity is reduced to the letter "A" and whose constant denial of an attraction toward other men is based not on acts performed or not but on a refusal to name them and thereby to accept an identity for himself—Sebastián is a subject in search of representation.[2] While the national community, whose members collectively imagine themselves moving en masse through history from remote points of common origin to future shared utopias, assumes a triumphal voice to tout its tale, Sebastián's quest is to produce what Marjorie Garber has termed a "cultural legibility" (25) for the unheard, to create a presence where society perceives (and reinforces) an absence. This is no search to return to and restore an earlier (lost) state of bliss, but rather a burning need to strike out toward the future by unmasking the present. In this character's own words, "es necesario dejar constancia de lo vivido" (one must leave behind [some] evidence of one's life experiences) (14). Zapata's text is composed of Sebastián's attempts to create visible, comprehensible, and material proof of an *histoire* denied, to find a way, at least for the moment and in this specific context, to represent the story of a flesh-and-blood individual struggling with (and against) the "milagro mexicano" (Mexican [social and economic] miracle) at every turn. When public rhetoric fades out, personal *historias* take over. And when traditional expectations of "legibility" are confused and confounded by the perfection of strategies of deception, then social "anxiety" (a term used by Garber in the subtitle of her book) is provoked as a result. Not only is the emperor denounced as clothed only in the deceptive garb of patriarchy and nationalism, but the body that has been (or could be) hidden underneath holds out a few unexpected (illegible?) surprises of its own.

The contents of Sebastián's diary embody the search for a form in which to convey his turbulent feelings and experiences, which do not seem to fit the conventional heterosexual love story mold with its repertoire of models of identity and conduct to emulate. Instead, he manages to perform what Doty calls "queer" readings (2) of commercial films and the sentimental lyrics of popular songs, thereby appropriating their contents for his own situation. So he creates an allegiance between himself and gay-identified singer Juan Gabriel, just to mention one example. While the social deception of reading these lyrics as straight, simultaneously denying or repressing their performance by someone who is not, is a convenient commonplace tactic of a patriarchal state,[3] Sebastián's disruption of this so-called harmony of legibility ends its dogmatic reign. Accepted, sanctioned (in other words, straight) love stories are chronicled by the cultural mainstream in systematic form to compile a public record of its own successes and triumphs. This is documented clearly in texts ranging from comic books to *telenovelas* (soap operas), from B movies to "high culture" works of literature (novels, poems, plays), and from popular music to prestigious literary awards and prizes for praiseworthy versions of requited love. On the other hand, stories of so-called dangerous, aberrant, abnormal—to paraphrase Garber, "illegible"—desires, those subjected to constant obstacles and threats by the denizens of social homogeneity and conformity, are presented in *En jirones* as infinitely more challenging and rewarding to represent. The challenge comes from the necessity to create alternate forms of expression because the "tradition" of public storytelling by gay men and lesbians is at best problematic; the reward is the articulation of identity and critique through disruptive hybrid narratives. These narratives, with their personal and intimate "historias," seriously call into question the superficial harmony of the heterosexual family romance on the level of national discourse. This is a fact Sebastián recognizes when he observes that "los amores afortunados no tienen historia: si acaso crónica; no hay nada relevante en la inconsciente modorra de la felicidad" (happy love stories have no tale to tell: maybe only a chronicle of events; there is nothing illustrious or outstanding in the unconscious drowsiness of sheer bliss) (112). The individual whose life and desires are in complete harmony with the goals that have been promoted and institutionalized by the nation—values such as marriage, family, heterosexuality, and religious orthodoxy—repeats a recognizably comfortable litany of acts, ones Sebastián reads as fraudulent, alienating, and "irrelevant" to his own life. The privileging of this ideal of sameness, as well as its implicit personification in all members of society, is the lie perpetuated in and through narrative accounts of the divine state of bliss just mentioned. Perched as he is on the margins—we could call them more accurately the extremities—of the social body, Sebastián finds in the realm of popular film and music a promisingly dynamic space of opposition in which to contest such a vision of cultural unanimity and homogeneity. It is his appropriation of these facets of public culture that both gives substance to his writings (therapeutic acts on paper

recommended by a psychiatrist) and leads him to an awareness of the inconsistencies between the lyrics of popular love songs or the stilted dialogue of
a film script and his own emotional devastation by his problematic relationship with "A." The metaphysics of love on the screen—the coming together of
opposing forces (and genders) to join in idyllic completeness—and the physical aspects of very real desire do not merge as one seamless unity but instead
couple in bouts of irreconcilable violence. The "horror" of the text, Garber's
social and cultural "anxiety" carried to the extreme, is produced out of such
encounters between what Kristeva calls "the clean and proper body" and the
abject or monstrous body whose legibility has not remained intact (Creed 11).
The boundaries set up between the healthy and the loathsome or repulsive
(according to social taboos) are the breeding grounds for the embodiment of
society's most deeply ingrained fears, for as Creed reminds us, "the monstrous
is produced at the border which separates those who take up their proper gender roles from those who do not" (11).

As critic John Fiske points out, this space of the popular is "contradictory
and conflictual to its core" (2). Owing to the fact that the making of popular
culture is just that, a *process* by which those consumers disenfranchised from
the production of images, discourses, and objects in the marketplace appropriate those very resources from the social system's centers of media power
to recirculate these modified artifacts in new contexts of opposition, so popular "goods" belong to two constituencies simultaneously: those "inside" and
those "outside" economic and cultural agencies. The "outsiders" are cultural
"have-nots" in a sense, even if they have a modicum of financial security, because they do not find themselves reflected in the images associated with their
society's national identity. Such an appropriation occurs, then, in response to
actual "lived bodies" (O'Neill 23) and individual stories, rather than to the
idealized market version of Mexican life. By incorporating into a parodic narrative selected traces of the very media images that promote and maintain
an artificially happy consensus for the "afortunados" (those lucky in love and
felicitously celebrated in the media), the popular is involved in a never-ending
struggle to explode standard readings and produce new ones (by the "desafortunados," or the emotionally and erotically "unlucky" and invisible, one
assumes). These rereadings, or alternative readings,[4] of mass culture texts and
icons (faces or objects identifiable by their association with certain traits or
characteristics) come strikingly close to what Doty proposes as the counter-

reception of the popular by those who do not identify with the exclusionary classifications contained in these texts and images. He proposes instead a "nonstraight" or "queer" (2) position with respect to their reception, displacing the original relations (and relationships) of the elements in the text. Such "rearrangements" speak both to so-called mainstream consumers and to marginal members of the social body, but they speak to them in different ways. For some, they are unorthodox "perversions" or "inversions" of what is assumed to be consensus reality (husband-wife-child, for example, or man-woman), while for others they signify a power to reorder or control things that is normally absent from daily life. Thus, for instance, real-life Mexican screen star Angélica María and musical performer Juan Gabriel become the touchstones for imagining an alternative identity for Zapata's characters, from *En jirones* through his subsequent novels. Each media star has an "original" audience of fans and admirers as well as an "alternative" following. For one group, the stars are idealized abstractions of complete acculturation; for the other, they become a projection of illegitimate and putatively illegible desires.

From the throwaway images of popular culture, images meant to be consumed and immediately discarded as cultural waste, Zapata elaborates a number of texts whose characters not only salvage these figures to recycle them in rereadings by the socially and sexually "unfortunate," but also confer upon them a status far beyond the images originally produced, and longer-lasting as well in their constantly mutating reappearances. Zapata's versions of Angélica María, actor and singer Enrique Guzmán, and performer Juan Gabriel surpass even the media's superstar cults: they have become reigning deities of a fictional universe enthralled by the production and consumption of such figures and their potential for rereadings. It is this very same cultural process of creating taste—the acceptable, the desired, the decent versus the scorned, the vilified, the reprobate—as well as the results of such polarization that are scrutinized by Zapata through the use of camp.[5] This usage corresponds in particular to what Andrew Ross has written about the camp aesthetic: "Camp is a rediscovery of history's waste. Camp irreverently retrieves not only that which had been excluded from the serious high-cultural 'tradition' but also the more unsalvageable material that has been picked over and found wanting by purveyors of the 'antique' " (13–14).[6] In a so-called developing country such as Mexico in which the work of the *pepenadores,* or garbage pickers, is a recognized activity if not an actual profession, the camp aesthetic of cultural scavenging and revalorizing appears to find a perfect niche. And by recirculating these cultural "waste products," by now supposedly emptied of meaning and value according to bourgeois tastes, in unexpected and conflictual contexts, the writer also uncovers all of the possibilities of the salvage worker who dives into the murky depths of the national cultural past to dredge up moments and images reborn in scandalous fury, flying in the face of "decency" and "quality," as luminous beacons for the alternative stories, the individual's takes on the present. Camp's use of momentary glimpses, sporadic gestures, chance encounters, and reversed images allows for a plethora of alternative readings that disrupt dominant codes of spectatorship and consumption. Those who previously decoded signs and meanings produced by ostensibly mainstream storytellers work with the traces and residues of those tales to recast them into spectacles intended to engender a new sense of community in an excluded group and to expose the illusion of neutral images that really are ideological ones. The stylized glamour of camp figures generates a different sense of pleasure in a cultural presence, creating a "queer aura" (Meyer 16) on this new work of art that brings the dead historical "waste" back forcefully into the realm of the living and the present.

In Zapata's 1989 novel *La hermana secreta de Angélica María* (The secret sister of Angélica María) we come face to face with the cinematic chronicles of the lives and loves of real-life screen actress Angélica María through the perspective of the narrated tale(s) of a character in triple masquerade. None of the character's identities is fixed or "natural"; each is discovered by the reader as the product of a social idea or myth. First as Alvaro (a hermaphroditic figure who dreams of being the actress's twin), then as transvestite singer Alba María ("la del sexo de los ángeles" [she with the sex of the angels], 113), and finally as transsexual Alexina ("la mujer de lava y fuego" [the woman of lava and fire], 126) who aspires to incorporate into real life the celluloid images of the fairy tales represented on the silver screen, this character reacts to the daily bombardment of popular culture in ways mainstream (heterosexual) Mexico never expects. Taking the actress's dramatized stories at face value and making kitsch and pastiche the aesthetic orders of the day, Zapata's text parodies the artificial paradise of musical films' "unconscious state of happiness" ("la inconsciente modorra de la felicidad," as cited earlier) that is fed on a daily basis to a primed and avid consumer public. This parody of so-called acceptable taste is accomplished by following the narrative trail of Alvaro/Alba/Alexina, who internalizes the images of an idealized femininity acted out on the stage or screen by this cult star to take those images to their logical conclusion. As Westmoreland aptly sums it up: "An individual without an identity, Alvaro attempts to find one through a relationship with the cinema" (51).

From fallen innocent to resident of a psychiatric ward, through a modern Mexican landscape littered with monstrous (illegible? marginal?) inhabitants, haunting nightmares, and the agony of repressed passions, an alternative story is created—a "petite histoire" whose narrating subject manages to confront and expose many of the cultural myths presented as natural fact, including an essentialist notion of the masculine and the feminine. To do so, it appears that Alvaro has heeded well the advice of his literary predecessor Sebastián to "asumi[r] la cursilería como consigna" (take up vulgarity as your standard) (107). This conscious assumption of exaggerated bad taste is pure camp; his goal is literally to become an image of the feminine figure idolized by Angélica María's fans, down to the last physical detail of this "culturally ubiquitous" figure, as the pop cult icon Madonna has been called (Schwichtenberg 1). Since the actress is endowed with an obvious "cultural legibility" for an entire previous generation of Mexican moviegoers, Alvaro has made a good (if ironic) choice of icon for himself. And his rereading of her identity creates a new conjunction of contentious fragments that echoes Alvaro's own divided self; both are "tainted" by the monstrosity of difference. This is where our story really begins, since this is the point at which Alvaro steals the star off the screen by adopting her appearance and ventriloquizing her voice, setting in motion a crossover never meant to exist in everyday life. As Ross points out, camp "never proposes a *direct* relation between the conditions it speaks to [real life, the present] . . . and the discourse it speaks with—usually a bricolage of features pilfered from conditions of the past" (18). The breaching of this *imaginary* relation between historical moments, and between self and society, is the rupture set up in Zapata's text by Alvaro and his object of adoration, Angélica.

To be the "secret sister" of Angélica María, not merely another admirer but a "wanna-be" who fetishizes her image, small-town movie addict Alvaro must aspire to embody all the details of the storybook life represented on film by this Mexican version of the 1960s bubblegum teen heroine. In brutal contrast to the social and political clashes of that decade, one during which the federal government flaunted an exemplary model of social progress and economic development under the national banner of the 1968 Olympic Games but that ended with the massacre in Tlatelolco that same year, the character

Angélica María inhabits an artificial paradise. For official Mexico, she is the personification of an imaginary wholeness and unity, the secret goddess of youth and the perfect antidote to cultural anxiety. Surrounded by imported racing cars, sporting expensive miniskirts, protagonist of harmless flirtations and marvelous adventures with predictable happy endings, this actress-now-character is presented as the icon of feminine perfection. As a commercial film star whose promotional material for mass audiences refers to her as "la novia de la juventud de toda América Latina" (the girlfriend of all Latin America's young people) — a refrain that appears scattered throughout the novel[7] — her image becomes the official model for the country's burgeoning youth industry, which is paving the way for their assimilation into society as adults. She also appears, in Zapata's literary version at least, as the saintlike protectress of the adolescent Alvaro (and, later, of aspiring star Alba María), who finds in her films an antidote for the sordidness of everyday life.

Feelings of alienation and estrangement from the tiny, hot, suffocating town and its insular inhabitants have left him numb and "disembodied," with neither a historical dimension (the family's roots) nor a personal identity culled from an actual "lived body," since he spends all his time secluded in movie theaters. His numbness is not the product of a lack of feeling, an insensitivity toward life, but of a perceived gap between an inner sensuality and an estranged body or surface on which to express it. In a general sense, Alvaro is haunted by the Freudian uncanny in his not feeling "at home" in his own body. This distance is established early in the story by the narrator, whose voice sets up the contrast between Angélica María as cultural icon and Alvaro/Alba/Alexina as an icon of bad taste (the queen of kitsch). We are told that, from the cinematic rhetoric of romance, Alvaro "ha aprendido actitudes y comportamientos diferentes de los de la mayoría de la gente que lo rodea" (has learned attitudes and behavior that differ from those of the majority of the people around him) (24), because the relationships between men and women on the screen don't correspond to what he encounters in everyday life. Preferring what he finds in the dark refuge of the theater to the relations between the sexes in the light of day, Alvaro chooses to fantasize about the world according to the dream factory of the movies. The narrator remarks: "desde hace mucho tiempo [Alvaro] tiene la impresión de que no es igual a sus condiscípulos. . . . Ya desde antes no compartía los intereses de los muchachos de su edad. . . . Ahora, la identificación con ellos ha desaparecido casi por completo: no sonríe

ni se excita con las fotos de cuerpos desnudos que algunos llevan en carteri-
tas. . . . No, definitivamente él no es así" (for a long time now [Alvaro] has had
the impression that he isn't the same as the rest of his schoolmates. . . . Even
from long before he had never shared the interests of the boys his age. . . . Now,
any identification with them has disappeared almost completely: he doesn't
smile nor does he get excited by the photos of nude bodies that some of them
carry in their wallets. . . . No, he definitely isn't like that) (51). The abyss that he
feels opening up between himself and the rest of the male adolescents in town
places Alvaro at the mercy of taunts and threats, leading him to enshrine his
object of adoration, Angélica María, even further as a model for the recovery
of the lost (repressed) part of himself. He finds consolation by constructing an
altar to her in his grandmother's home — a shrine to "[la] muchacha decente,
católica, bien educada" (the decent, Catholic, well-mannered young woman)
(35) who is represented on the screen. This act of idolatry and narcissism (since
he is her wanna-be) is stimulated by his grandmother's own interweaving of
fiction and fact, life and film, within those very walls to create a perfect atmosphere for the germination of his fantasies and the "pura combustión interna"
(pure internal combustion) (42–43) the adolescent Alvaro experiences every
night under the sheets when his imagination runs free. Between the poles of
the doting matriarch and the protective feminine talisman, Alvaro experiences
traumatic physical changes he must struggle to deal with and overcome or accept. The basis of his alternative identity in a body ruled by competing codes
of biology and gender alignment is found, as one might expect, in film.

Each facet of this character is trapped in a physical body that is never at
peace with itself, but is rather the constant source of treasonous acts and "repulsive reminders" (33, 38, 39) of its actual biology, a situation the narrator
constantly refers to as "el Problema Insoluble" (the Unsolvable Problem) (113,
119). With this characterization of Alvaro/Alba, Zapata sets up a warring encounter between opposing body parts and desires, not the ideal archetype of
the androgynous figure reminiscent of some lost mythical beauty and perfection (the union of opposites in dynamism and vitality). The "abnormal" (Weil
10) or monstrous joining of male and female in one hermaphroditic body does
not suggest symmetry or complementarity, but excess (see Weil 36), instability,
and divisiveness. An "excess" of such nature, the "extra" organs beyond what is
read (legible) as a state of "normality," seems to echo the excessiveness of camp
exaggeration; it is also indicative of a purposeful confusion of transparent

identity and the comfortable reliance on traditional codes of cultural legibility.[8]

In the case of hermaphrodite Alvaro/Alba María, the presence of a female organ is the source of rejection by other adolescents, who are interested in comparing and judging the physical attributes of their male anatomy; on the other hand, tabloid reporter and would-be rapist Alberto Muñiz reacts with horror and revulsion when he discovers Alba María's most intimate secret — her male organ. What appeared "legible" at first glance was confused and clouded by closer firsthand inspection. Both moments of epiphany lead to the violent elimination of the source of rejection (or of threatened violation), playmate Toño in the first instance and aggressive media hound Alberto in the second. Friend-turned-foe Toño is thrown off a cliff and made to disappear for good; in the latter case, after castrating the aggressor, Alba dons Alberto's clothing to "pass" as a man and escape detection as the murderer. So while Alberto and Toño fail to "read" the identity of Alba/Alvaro with accuracy, the latter also is taken in by appearances (the bosom buddy; the reporter interested in furthering the career of the ingenue). When the veil is lifted, the only possible outcome is violence, for blissful endings and unambiguous identifications occur with regularity on screen but not necessarily off. In Alvaro/Alba's own words, "La vida es pocas veces una superproducción. . . . Su técnica es torpe . . . ; abundan las tomas sobreexpuestas . . . ; y los movimientos de los labios no siempre están en sincronía con el sonido" (Life is rarely a superproduction. . . . Its technique is clumsy . . . ; too many shots are overexposed . . . ; and the movements of the lips aren't always synchronized with the sound) (101).

Each incarnation of the character, in addition, must confront daily what Susan Bordo calls the culture industry's "plastic discourse" (275). This refers to the fact that a consensus of cultural legibility is contingent on specific codes of both appearance and behavior. The sources of these include television advertisements, radio commercials, billboards, magazines, newspapers, and all other media that reflect dominant norms of body imagery, including silicone-injected fantasy breasts, elective cosmetic surgery, aerobicized and weight-trained hardbodies, and smooth, unblemished adolescent faces packaged alongside the remedial treatments needed to obtain the very same look of "perfection." Following such guidelines reduces the character's chances of provoking societal anxiety in others over his/her identity. In his striving to fulfill the goal of actually incarnating Angélica María in a life—his lived body as homage to her virtues—patterned after some or, if the truth be told, all of her movie roles wrapped up in one, Alvaro decides that any amount of personal sacrifice is worth the achievement of such an outcome. He becomes convinced that "nadie se arrepiente de ser una mujer completa" (no one regrets being a complete [and total] woman) (117). Thus arises his/her recourse to *techne,* all possible modes of art or artifice used to enhance, or mask, the "natural" and achieve the look of "total femininity." For him at least, Angélica María literally embodies in flesh and blood an idealized and unproblematical "feminine," the improbable combination of virgin and seductress that is unworkable and unfeasible in real Mexican society. Only in the *jouissance* of his double (hermaphroditic) desire could the two—innocence and experience, in the movie versions—commingle in one body.

When Zapata has his character assume the appearance and behavior of this cult idol, both the dangers and the profits of taking on such an identity are brought to light through exaggeration and irony. Popular singer/performer Madonna's "Material Girl" recording and video, a pastiche version of Marilyn Monroe's character Lorelei from the film *Diamonds Are a Girl's Best Friend,* is similar in its intent to question through parody the automatic connections between erotic and economic capital. Yet Alba María goes far beyond by crossing over and combining gender roles (Madonna remains the mere simulacrum of a doubtful seductress). In each case, what was a relatively innocent and naive gold-digging fantasy in the original version turns into premeditated narcissism and posturing in the second. The resulting "monstrosity" of the camp rereading is obviously much more powerful in Alvaro/Alba than the peek-a-boo teasing of Madonna. All vestige of seriousness is gone from the first, while the Material Girl yearns (unsuccessfully, for the most part) to be "taken seriously." Yet the comparison is not gratuitous, for each figure serves as an icon of materiality for the culture in (and by) which it is produced. As Suzanna Walters remarks in the introduction to her discussion of feminist cultural theory, Madonna's constant recreation of herself, from precocious teenager to Blonde Ambition dominatrix, has triggered parallel rereadings of her image on the part of the public and critics alike. The same might be said for Alvaro/Alba's appropriation of Angélica María. Walters writes, "Accompanying Madonna's own elaboration of superstardom has been a sustained effort—by the mass media and academics alike—to continually produce and reproduce this cultural icon. Madonna circulates constantly in the cultural practices of everyday life, from lurid *National Enquirer* exposés to the serious cultural scholarship that has been dubbed 'Madonna-ology.' . . . The figure of Madonna is emblematic of the confused way women are represented in popular culture . . . [and] different audiences may interpret the same images in various ways. One group's 'negative' image may be another's source of empowerment" (2–3). For movie addict Alvaro, the bubblegum-chewing girl-next-door mainstream idol becomes the model for Alba María, his own "impersonation" of Angélica María.

All of the trappings and paraphernalia needed to square his external appearance with the idealized form on the movie screen, then, correspond to Alvaro's assumption of a "hyperfeminine" identity as Alba María. In fact, all of the accoutrements, cosmetics, and biotechnology available to carry out this utopian project feed such a desire to change and improve, to defy the body's material limits, to "live the fantasy," as Chanel's commercial constantly reminds us. For Alvaro/Alba/Alexina, Angélica María becomes the camp "paradigm of plasticity" (Bordo 266) and the model of self-transformation, an identification whose paradoxes in reproducing patterns of desire (young, thin, blonde, heterosexual, etc.) Zapata plays out to the utmost in this text. We must remember, after all, that in order for Alba and/or Alexina to be liberated from the body of Alvaro she must be enslaved to the identity of Angélica María — a point of reference whose identity is already a performance, a simulacrum of reality, an artifice of film production. The result is that femininity takes on the role of the ultimate in commodity fetishes for Alvaro/Alba; it is something that acquires an intrinsic value above and beyond mere "exchange" (as it would have in cinematic portrayal) and whose symbolic value resides in the realm of surplus and exaggeration. In this parody of the iconization of commercial movie stars and polarized gender categories, amid the free play of the elements of fashion by which identities are put on and removed at will with each outfit, sex reassignment surgery and medical practices involving body transformation seem to function on equal ground. Whereas the use of specific articles of clothing such as miniskirts and go-go boots, blonde wigs, skin lotions, perfumes, and makeup signals the transition between the roles of innocent Esperanza and experienced Brenda for Angélica María in the film *Cinco de chocolate y uno de fresa* (Five scoops of chocolate and one of strawberry) (1967), for instance, here body parts become another kind of fashion accessory, changeable to match the shifting search for identity and to celebrate the splintered subject. Where everything is a question of construction and not "nature," all façades can be torn down and their components regrouped or reassembled. This individual subject is no longer presented as unified but instead as more of a general site for the schizophrenic encounter of roles and fantasies (see Berg 67). Moreover, Dr. Angel Morán, the surgeon in charge of the operation to "sort out" the character's identity once and for all (an ironic quest that *must* end in failure, of course), views Alvaro/Alba as a personal challenge to come up with an unblemished *creation;* it is his one big chance to be in control of a scientific procedure that culminates in a "perfect" biological female. As if to seal her fate, he refers to his creation as "la Verdadera, . . . la que enloquecerá de pasión a todos los hombres" (the One True Woman, . . . the one who will drive men crazy with desire) (126). Such a triumph of the medical institution's authority over lived bodies (and their "monstrous" sexualities, one assumes) maximizes the camp effect of the text in its idolatry of body parts and their capacity to be recycled as so many more cultural artifacts.

Alvaro's intense and overwhelming obsession with popular culture's chronicle of heterosexual love stories leads him to attempt a transfer of those images over into the realm of his own everyday life as Alba. But at this point he makes the surprising discovery that, as far as he is concerned at least and as the narrator has known all along, "en la vida real [tales] sentimientos no tienen cabida" (in real life [such] feelings have no place) (24). The complication does not stem from Alvaro's identification with a media image but from his casting himself in the role of the "wrong" character, the venerated "Novia" (his references to her always appear with a capital letter, as the archetype of the "girlfriend") and not one of her leading men such as teen idol Enrique Guzmán. After worshiping at the altar of her photographed image and practicing her signature obsessively until there is little or no difference between the original version and the wanna-be's, Alvaro also learns to imitate her voice and singing style. He aims first to carry out his dream of following her down the road to stardom as enticingly promised by her films, then to turn himself into her double in "real" life. To indicate this crossover dream, Zapata suggestively titles one of the novel's episodes "Mi vida es una canción" (My life is a song), simultaneously echoing the title of a film starring his idol and underscoring Alvaro's undying devotion to living out the message of the lyrics.

As the young Alvaro, then as Alba, and finally as the exaggerated Alexina, a woman who derives intense pleasure and self-affirmation from the hedonistic enjoyment of her public image by the male audience as long as a certain amount of protective distance is maintained between them, this complex character ends up victimized by the violence of contemporary society through such acts of cruelty as assault and attempted rape. First a childhood friend, then fellow music performers on tour with her, then press agents–turned–road groupies all follow this pattern of violence toward an individual who plays the role of feminine ideal so well that s/he becomes the victim of her/his own success. In each case, the uncovering of identity as masquerade—whether by Toño in the gymnasium locker room, by a hapless mariachi in a run-down motel, or by a so-called celebrity interviewer in his apartment—brings with it corresponding acts of vengeance, committed by both Alvaro and Alba in the name of their moral guiding light, Angélica María. The constant paradox is the fact that these men all uncover the "secret" of Alba/Alvaro as an identity constructed on outward "legibility" and internal contradiction, but they fail to consider themselves (and their "masculinity") in the same light. As a result of this persistent feeling of being stalked and the perpetual threat of being "discovered" (as someone whose biology complicates his or her apparent gender identity), the narrating subject's most pressing desire moves from the realm of corporal presence and public spectacle to the private wish for disembodiment. From all (in one body), we are presented with the alternative of none (absence). Alba dreams of being a free-floating signifier in the most literal sense, a subject not tied down in any way: "olvidar tu cuerpo . . . si se pudiera. Ser otra o, de plano, no ser" (to forget your body . . . if only you could. To be someone else or, to put it plainly, not to be at all) (42); "mi único sueño es no ser yo" (my only dream is not to be myself) (121). The wish for difference, for permanent "otherness" in which there would be no fixed identity at all, locates this subject outside any one single body or conventional representation of that body, placing it instead squarely in the realm of fantasy. The character would then inhabit only the hyperreality of the larger-than-life figures on the movie screen, whose contradictions, disillusionments, and frustrations always fade out with the final credits.

Rather than accept what Fiske has distinguished as a two-poled structure set up by patriarchal culture in which, in his words, "fantasy is often seen as feminine, whereas representation [that is, cultural legibility and materiality, to cite Garber once again] is associated with the masculine" (123), with the former considered escapist and therefore lacking what the latter wields as "real" political power to make sense of the world and to carve out one's place in it, Zapata's characters tap into the potential oppositionality of fantasy as an alternative form of representation within the very same boundaries of society. Self-representation and fantasy inform one another; each is an aspect of the social subject much as Angélica María,[9] as the image of a cultural utopia, incites Alvaro to act on his own fantasies of desire. The interactive process unleashes a series of events that prove, beyond a shadow of a doubt, the tangible effects of fantasy on the everyday world, just as the opposite has already been proved true in society's projection of an ideal onto the figure of film actress Angélica María. In other words, Angélica María on screen is the catalyst that puts into motion Alvaro's acting out his "secret sisterhood" as compensation for the rejections of "real life." The end result, however, is a society that reinforces the idealized cinematic vision of femininity while disavowing any public space to carry it through, especially in the guise of someone as disruptive and socially contentious as Alvaro/Alba. S/he is the source of intense cultural anxiety.

The intrusion of the camp aesthetic in the presentation of this character is Zapata's way of narrating this ambiguity and conflict back into the field of public representation. How else might we explain, for instance, the creation of the transsexual Alexina in terms of a new Eve, the ultimate recycling of an icon of femininity (whose principal traits are seduction and treason, of course) turned back on itself by the triumph of science over nature (and religion, obviously)? Eve is the zero degree of the feminine and the physical embodiment of Alvaro's acknowledged wish to *be* a perfect representation while at the same time to *parody* the power of representation by accepting Dr. Angel Morán's offer to give him a rebirth, "hacer de ti la mujer de tus sueños" (make you into the woman of your dreams) (121). But are they *his* dreams, or do they come from another source? Purity and seductive perfection are thus reconfigured as technological or clinical improvements and not naturally occurring attributes. These are dreams planted and nourished by media images, now being taken quite literally.

Moving freely between a culture and its fantasies in his/her various incarnations, described in terms of the multiple cameras Alba María imagines focused on her from long-shot angles that track her daily activities (104), Alvaro/Alba/Alexina dares to attempt to make social reality live up to its dreams and myths. S/he challenges the paradigmatic "love story" to come true for every member of the body politic, that "very flesh of society" (23) that O'Neill construes as the conjunction of experiences of *all* the individual lived bodies that make up a collectivity. In short, the tale of this "secret sister" accomplishes precisely what Sebastián yearns for in *En jirones:* to leave a legacy of life experiences that do not necessarily conform to the social and sexual mainstream. But this is done by using the cultural and sexual myths at the very core of that mainstream. Yet what is left behind are the incongruous traces of pastiche, not tragedy (as a social community might wish on its supposedly aberrant fringes) but the incessant and aleatory realignment of a postmodern subject with whatever fragments of cultural debris it might come across. "Lo vivido" (lived experience; what is lived) is conditioned by "lo visto" (what is seen; what one perceives) in the popular press and film. These are images and relations that, when taken at face value, can lead only to contradiction, failure, and madness. In order to succeed as Angélica María (or as a reasonable facsimile), Alvaro/Alba therefore must be presented by the tongue-in-cheek narrator as "crazed" by the media and "going mad" trying to live up to the role of the perfect woman at the mercy of her adoring (male) fans. The irony is that s/he must fail grandiosely in this "voyage out" in order for the story of the text to be successful in its camp commentary.

It is telling that Zapata chooses to end the novel with postoperative Alexina sequestered in the psychiatric ward on the top floor of a public hospital, feeling that the only "reality" with which she is in touch is mental, no longer physical. As she imagines herself on the ultimate film set of her acting career, with a famous director calling the shots for her every move (while he is actually the resident psychiatrist Armando Marenti, who keeps her in a drug-induced marginal twilight, as divorced from her physical body as she had wished to be earlier), Alexina's "lived experience" is transferred from outside to inside. We are told that "El cuerpo casi deja de existir, o se mueve de manera autónoma: las piernas ya no le pesan, las manos no le tiemblan, camina sin fatigarse, resiste el frío, el calor, la incomodidad. Sólo el cerebro tiene un volumen y un peso excesivos, como si de un día para otro hubiera crecido desmesuradamente y ahora necesitara más espacio para acomodarse sin ser oprimido" (Her body almost ceases to exist, or it moves along automatically: her legs seem weightless, her hands don't tremble, she walks without getting tired, she doesn't feel the cold, the heat, or any discomfort. Only her brain feels excessively large and heavy, as if from one day to the next it had grown tremendously and now needed more space to fit comfortably [in her head]) (149). This incessant and concentrated activity of the mind—fantasy, imagination, "locura," or whatever one might choose to call it—becomes her antidote to the "mundo en caos" (world in chaos) (149). Such a confused or chaotic world (society) promotes spectacles of pleasure, yet then unjustly denies them any practicable embodiment for *some* of its members (those who are "unfortunate," as Sebastián reminds us in *En jirones*). This taunting of individual drives for pleasure and fulfillment lives up to the concept of "spectacle" as surface, mere performance and display, something consumed by the eyes before they move on to the next visual target. This is how "cultural waste" is produced and how societies sustain their pacified consumers. Yet it also can serve as the context from which radical (or Merck's "deviant") rereadings emanate to cause a momentary chink in the armor of respectability and legibility. Appearances can no longer be taken for granted as unanimously readable according to some system of universal values.

And so it ends up that "esa hermana secreta que todos tenemos" (that secret sister we all have) (125) latent somewhere within us is simultaneously the personification of desire *and* of frustration. She is "[nuestra] hermana, pero también [nuestra] más feroz enemiga" (our sister, but our most fierce enemy as well) (151), because this object of desire so frequently remains just that—a passive object or a fantasy image or an unfulfilled wish, not an acting subject. Within a social reality constructed of institutionalized and codified relations between the dominant and the subordinate, the center and the margins, "los afortunados" and "los desafortunados," the lines are drawn clearly to divide those who get to live the fairy tale and those who don't. Not content to play the role of outcast to which s/he is relegated, Alvaro/Alba takes matters into her/his own hands and yet again tries to "cross over" and live the best of both worlds. When Alexina finally encounters Angélica María face to face outside the star's opulent home, she accuses the actress of selfishly blocking her own road to success. The meeting is destined to fail because it is evident that there is no accountability in life for promises made on screen, nor any connection between the actress and the actual flesh-and-blood person. (The confusion has driven more than one fan to acts of desperation and violence in their efforts to make the two worlds coincide.) When Alexina, "enloquecida" (driven to madness) (151) by her disillusionment with what she feels are the unfulfilled personal promises held out by this cult heroine, threatens her idol with physical harm, she must be stopped by the guardians of social order. Guards, police, and medical personnel step in. She has overstepped the bounds of proper and "decent" human relations and therefore must be removed to the place reserved by the state for those with such transgressive behavior: the psychiatric clinic. She has committed the unpardonable sin of mixing the discourses of reality and fantasy in the same realm, somewhat akin to Alvaro/Alba's "having it all" in terms of biological equipment; it is assumed that the two are not meant to coexist. She is literally out of place, having passed into the domain of the "real" woman Angélica María. It should come as no surprise, therefore, that the very next paragraph in the text opens with a sedated Alexina, under therapeutic treatment for such unacceptable transgressions, gazing out over the urban panorama from which she has been forcibly removed. The last touch of irony comes when she hears herself—still in the guise of the performer Alba María at an earlier recording session—singing popular tunes on the ward's portable radio. The disembodied voice, one that is and yet is not her, is the last remaining vestige of her direct contact with the world outside the hospital. And it is not a live performance but the technological reproduction of one. Ironically, Alba María has already ceased to exist as "real," for she too has become a pop icon like Angélica María before her.

The seemingly infinite variations on the story of the family's origins and personal history recited by Alvaro's grandmother in fervid rituals of (foundational) storytelling establish a counterpoint to the comprehensive, precise, and unwavering genealogy of the social body reflected in the official story of the nation. They also converge and contradict one another in ways similar to the variations in Alvaro/Alba. The stories end not in resolution but with promises of infinite mutations. Places, characters, and outcomes vary constantly. These are episodes whose hybrid contents intersperse with the parallel, and subsequently intersecting, tales of Alvaro and Alba, whose mutating images of feminine identity circulate throughout the narrative in sharp contrast to the scenes of women as static and complacent objects served up in popular films to please and sustain the fantasies of male spectators. (One of these very fantasies is, in fact, the coexistence of sexual innocence and experience in one female character, perhaps a reflection of the male and female components cohabiting in Alvaro/Alba.) In offering us such variable and unstable versions of personal life stories, *La hermana secreta de Angélica María* ridicules the power of the media as the great leveler of images by endlessly displacing them into different, disquieting, and disorienting contexts. The text itself explores the nature of ambiguity by means of this type of structure (much as Sebastián seeks a form in which to represent his experiences in *En jirones*). The self-identification of Alvaro with the public image of movie star Angélica María is the prime example, but this is a case only one step removed from that of aging actress Amanda Murillo's own hypnotic fascination with an image of perpetual youth, beauty, and traditional morality long out of sync with recent changes in modern Mexican society. Rather than insulating a social body from outside influences, especially in terms of cultural and economic "modernization," the media has become an arena for cultural invasion and competition. In her attempts to keep the "glories" of the national past alive, the character Murillo is much more tragic than Alvaro/Alba, for she is aware of the ephemeral nature of these values, whereas the narrator keeps Alvaro/Alba a true innocent. The possibility of retaining such a profound degree of "innocence" in contemporary society, however, is in itself a camp commentary, for it presupposes the cancellation of one half of a dialogue by sheer force of will and the use of the rest of the message (the media's part) against its own source (the media itself). In the end, Alexina can only hear her "own" voice (albeit in the guise of Alba, who herself imitates Angélica María) in the media — no one else's.

For all of the above reasons, Zapata's text might well be considered a provocative skirmish on the great battlefield of contemporary culture with its constant wars of identity politics. It is deployed as a reminder that the official stories of national harmony, along with their readily recognizable heroes and heroines, are maintained as such by the reinforcement of selective exclusion alongside the propagated illusion of democratic participation and cohesive social progress. All of the images that make up a society's ideals are not available to all admirers, as the protagonist (in any guise) has found out. And what is "cultural waste" to one segment of society is a valuable treasure to another, at least in the hyperbolic exaggeration of camp, where idols don't fade away but become brighter and more garish with age. Are Alvaro/Alba/Alexina's alternatives really reducible only to either pretense and travesty, or insanity? When Zapata re-evokes these ready-made images, they are converted into pure camp; if they were cultural archetypes the first time around, now they function as space-fillers of the absurd kind. Their auras of heroism are dissolved into a masquerade of theatrical makeup and perfected superficiality; Alba María is a better Angélica María than the "real" one, challenging even the concept of the original and the copy. The characters and their voices have become a performance of what Travers calls "life and language *italicized*" (129). Dialogue and description are reduced to clichés or tabloid headline catch phrases, then set off in bold capital letters in a revolt against any appearance of seriousness or a "decently" modulated tone of voice. Every statement turns tongue-in-cheek; besides, such theatricality induces monologues rather than dialogues or "rational" discourse, since its language is recycled from the spent screenplays of previous productions. "El Monstruo del Insomnio" (the Monster of Insomnia) (68), "la Manifestación Rubia" (the Blonde Apparition) (91), "la Sonrisa Ubicua" (the Ubiquitous Smile) (93), "el Paso Decisivo" (the Decisive Step) (125) are but several examples of this raised pitch and its emphasis on ridiculing what is presented as the "natural" course of events. These are also shorthand tags used by the popular press to identify "personalities" in the public eye who have been reduced to these minimally recognizable characteristics. Tabloid headlines are filled with such references, especially in the case of public figures such as media stars. And in Westmoreland's view such an "emblematic" (50) reduction to archetypal values or features is a central characteristic of camp.

The very instability of these subjects—Alvaro, Alba, and stage performer Alexina—allows them to float freely as a constant challenge to facile, universalizing, or essentializing categories of identity.[10] Such an "amor desafortunado," the secret love story between Alvaro and Angélica María that motivates this text, cannot be chronicled, then, but only recounted as a narrative story, according to the conventions of literature and not those of history. This is precisely the point where the rhetoric of camp comes into play, with its "love of the *unnatural* (unconventional? illegible?)" (Sontag 275; emphasis added) and its adoration of style and artifice, lurking behind the mask of a straightforward message in language or gesture. This is what Sontag refers to as the possibility of reading beyond a "straight" interpretation (281) of character, action, or plot. Therein lies the narrator's (and Alvaro's) "queer" reading of star Angélica María. And therein also lies the irony of Zapata's own nonstraight reading of the principal accusations against his groundbreaking 1979 novel *Las aventuras, desventuras y sueños de Adonis García, el vampiro de la colonia Roma* (*Adonis García, A Picaresque Novel*, 1981). While this earlier text's primary aesthetic "offense" was considered (by some) its having been written on the theme of homosexuality with too much "seriedad profesional" (professional seriousness) (Blanco 188), in *La hermana secreta de Angélica María* the writer revels in the "nonserious" exaggeration of seemingly uncontrolled and hyperbolic "femininity" as projected by Angélica María through the eyes of

Alvaro/Alba/Alexina. For this writer none of the mainstream categories of the respectful, dignified, serious work of art can qualify as the measure of the success or failure of a specific text. Here we find instead the deliberate flaunting of an alternative reading in which, as Sontag explains, "the essential element is seriousness, a seriousness *that fails*" (283; emphasis added). In Zapata's novel such values of cultural and moral seriousness are dethroned and trampled on by Alvaro, Alba, and even Amanda Murillo. They are then placed back on a pedestal in mock admiration, to be cited (almost always) between quotation marks and with ritualized disdain signaled by extravagant and pompous reverence. This camp experience becomes the pleasure of the text, a popular alternative to the lessons on morality and "decency" propagated for mass audiences through the populist commercial cinema of the 1960s and beyond.

Working with the elements at hand, having Alvaro and Alba come together to form the new figure of seduction Alexina (Eve), the writer positions this narrative on the threshold of a new era, one that includes—as it inevitably must in today's world of global "progress and modernity"—all manner of technological interventions and biological innovations that render conventional categories of gender (and even humanity, given the advent of cyborgs, replicants, and androids) obsolete. That they were never "givens" of nature is one of the crucial points of Zapata's novel, for out of the vortex of origin myths told and retold by the grandmother comes neither masculine nor feminine progeny, but Alvaro/Alba, the performance of both in one singular individual. And that the models for his/her gender identity come from the cinema, parodying a traditional source of national social equilibrium and indoctrination, is a constant reminder of the tenuous borders between propriety and monstrosity. This is just another way of saying that difference does not divide but unites all of society, not in the artificiality of official harmony and bliss, but instead in healthy ambiguity, through the shared secret sisters contained in each and every individual.

Notes

1 As Victor Ouimette has observed of Unamuno's emphasis on individual consciousness as opposed to the "historical cataclysms [that] roll almost unnoticed over daily life" (22), self-image and inner awareness do battle with larger cultural issues in personal versions or private reenactments of such national social tensions. Ouimette

summarizes Unamuno's basic concept as follows: "his ideas of heroism were not predicated on historical figures raised against the backdrop of political or military accomplishments and illumined by repression and illusion, but simply on the ability of ordinary men to succeed in the tasks they had set for themselves, and despite obstacles that might appear" (22). While it is certain that gay men and lesbians were the subjects farthest from Unamuno's mind when he developed his theories of history and narration—nor is Zapata interested in the concept of the "heroic" lives of his characters—the struggles of the lone individual(s) against the pressures of the social collectivity would most definitely qualify as tactics for the survival (and recognition) of inner history in the face of threatened obliteration or absorption by the grandiose melodramas aimed at preserving the illusion of a greater homogeneous national image.

2   Sebastián writes in his "Diario de un enamorado" (Diary of a man in love), the text that composes the first section of the novel: "Mientras no tenga [él] que nombrar sus actos, decir sus sentimientos, no hay problema: su homosexualidad no existe" (As long as [he] doesn't have to label what he does or put his feelings into words, there's no problem: his homosexuality doesn't exist) (51). There is another aspect to this situation as well: the fact that in Latin American cultures the "active" subject in a physical relationship between two men generally is not considered homosexual, while the "passive" subject is. During their intense sexual encounters, "A" vehemently resists Sebastián's attempts to vary their acts of pleasure by a reversal of roles, thereby avoiding the categorizing of his sexuality as "gay." Parker summarizes this vision: "Within the terms of this cultural frame, relations between men are structured along the same lines as those between men and women, that is, in terms of sex and power. It is possible, though certainly not unproblematical, for a man to enter into sexual relations not only with women but also with other biological males without really sacrificing his fundamentally masculine identity. In taking the active role of penetration . . . , his hierarchical dominance is preserved" (47). The "passive" partner functions symbolically in a feminine role, but at the same time is seen as a biologically inferior copy of a woman or an "artificial" as opposed to "natural" one.

3   Of the relationship between *machismo* and the concept of national unity as represented in Mexican film, Berg writes, "*Machismo* is the name of the mutual agreement between the patriarchal state and the individual male in Mexico. Through it the individual acts out an implicit, socially understood role—*el macho*—which is empowered and supported by the state. The state in turn is made powerful by the male's identification with and allegiance to it" (107). Any flirtation with a confusion of categories or identities might lead the *macho* to have to confront everything he (or the state) stands for, the very foundations of an organic conception of hierarchy and the inequality of power.

4   Mandy Merck uses the term "perverse" or "deviant" readings in an obvious parody
     of such restrictive and proscriptive categorizations. Merck clarifies: "the title [of my
     book] *Perversions* has a bearing, for it declares that these are *readings, versions.* . . .
     That is to say: these readings are very often counters to other readings and do not
     themselves pretend to authority or finality, being in the main deliberate provoca-
     tions to replies, retorts, and further readings" (5). The plurality of readings, in the
     case of Zapata's characters, speaks to a similar provocative aspect of interpretation
     and an identification with a specific reading public, group, or segment of the social
     community.

5   Though the tactics and qualities of camp are so obviously fundamental to all of
     Zapata's texts, Westmoreland is the only critic outside Mexico to address this sub-
     ject in detail. In Mexico, camp as a narrative device (or artistic construct) has not
     been the subject of any critical studies on contemporary culture, at least to date.
     On the one hand, one might be tempted to speculate on the origins of camp in
     consumer societies, a (doubtful) status accorded Mexico only very recently and
     therefore still alien to discussions of cultural products and artifacts. On the other
     hand, the potentially rich confluences of masquerade, spectacle, and mask (even à
     la Octavio Paz and his essays on La Malinche) suggest future avenues of exploration
     in narrative, theater, and the arts.

6   In his challenging and well-argued introduction to *The Politics and Poetics of Camp*,
     Meyer points to this very idea of "historical waste" in very specific terms. In the
     section entitled "The queer as historical waste" he proposes that the invisibility
     of homosexuality, its absence or erasure from dominant codes of representation,
     signals the camp recovery of such trashed identity as gay practice (praxis) par ex-
     cellence (11–18).

7   Since 1993, the pop singer Lucero has inherited this title for a new generation of
     adolescents. The torch of the feminine has been passed, but Angélica María con-
     tinues to shine as a middle-aged icon of motherhood and respectability in the tele-
     vision soap opera "Agujetas de color de rosa" (Pink shoelaces).

8   Weil finds the icon of the hermaphrodite representative of the ultimate question-
     ing of paradigmatic oneness: "To examine the figure of the androgyne . . . is to
     discern the absent presence of another figure, that of the hermaphrodite, haunting
     the ideal of androgyny and its ordered, symmetrical opposition of male and female
     with the notion of an original confusion or chaos of sexes and desires. To bring
     this other figure onto the scene of representation is to subvert the text's structure
     of opposition and its use as a paradigm for the creation of meaning and hierarchy"
     (11). The imposition of a masculine or masculinist paradigm on the unity of the an-
     drogynous figure implies and sustains the inferiority of its "other" and of the halves
     separated with the loss (or mythical fall) of this ideal. To bring the hermaphrodite

out of the shadows breaks down this relationship of inequality through its reference to chaotic, and not blissfully harmonious, origins. The coupling of the desires
of the hermaphrodite is dynamic and irreconcilably violent.

9   The relationship between movie star and flesh-and-blood person is, to state the
obvious, problematic; one justifiably might wonder whether they are still distin-
guishable from one another at all times or whether all identity has been subsumed
under her screen roles. In that case, Alvaro/Alba is working on the premise of such
a reductionist view.

10 It appears to be no accident whatsoever that Zapata's most recent novel entitled
¿Por qué mejor no nos vamos? (Why don't we just pick up and leave?) (1992), is a
parody of the road-movie genre, consisting entirely of a free-flowing dialogue between two voices identified only as belonging to a "feminist" and to a homosexual.
Both have just turned forty, neither is given a name, and they are never actually
described physically in the pages of the text, perhaps pointing the way toward the
next narrative stage of identity after Alexina. Instead, their storytelling adventures
and endless tales of sexual encounters structure the narrative to form rituals of
splintered identity. The real or imagined exploits (just which are which is never
established, nor would such a distinction be a prerequisite in this fictional world)
are told on the move, in perpetual motion. The answer to the question posed by
the title seems always to be, as the narrative voices frequently repeat, "Bueno, sí.
Vámonos" (Sure, fine, let's go). There is never a lack of an imaginative response
when, in recurring bouts of insomnia, one voice or the other demands "cuéntame
algo" (tell me a story). Their tales never fail to produce the desired narcotic effect
on one another, followed by the dawning of a new day filled with the promises of
yet another episode to be shared as testimony to the actual or fantasized experiences of these characters. Alba María's wish to abandon the physical body for the
body of fantasy and illusion seems to have come true here. Being on the road is
just an excuse for narrating. One never arrives and never seems to have a final des-
tination in mind; in fact, the liminality of the voices is the only constant that ties
the tales together. Yet there is another aspect of these traveling stories that must be
underscored: it is that they all refer to the past, to a time of youth and innocence
and sexual energy (the 1960s and 1970s). From the characters' vantage point of the
1990s, the replay of these episodes as nothing more than a "búsqueda desencan-
tada" (disillusioned search) (Bautista 65) for what would, after the appearance of
AIDS and the renewed anti-gay sentiments of the late 1980s, increasingly look like
the impossibility of a "gay utopia" (Calva Pratt), crushes their promise and vitality.
Indeed, Bautista goes right to the heart of the matter when he calls *¿Por qué mejor
no nos vamos?* "una novela de náufragos" (a novel of shipwrecked lives) (65). It is
clearly a novel produced in a time of social and cultural transition.

Works Cited

Bautista, Juan Carlos. "Pasión y muerte de la literatura gay: Luis Zapata." *Viceversa* 4 (mayo/junio 1993): 63–65.

Berg, Charles Ramírez. *Cinema of Solitude: A Critical Study of Mexican Film, 1967–1983.* Austin: University of Texas Press, 1992.

Blanco, José Joaquín. "Zapata: el vampiro en los años del SIDA." In *Las intensidades corrosivas.* Villahermosa, Mexico: Gobierno del Estado de Tabasco, 1990. 187–193.

Bordo, Susan. " 'Material Girl': The Effacements of Postmodern Culture." In *The Madonna Connection: Representational Politics, Subcultural Identities, and Cultural Theory.* Ed. Cathy Schwichtenberg. Boulder, Colo.: Westview Press, 1993.

Creed, Barbara. *The Monstrous-Feminine: Film, Feminism, and Psychoanalysis.* London: Routledge, 1993.

Doty, Alexander. *Making Things Perfectly Queer: Interpreting Mass Culture.* Minneapolis: University of Minnesota Press, 1993.

Fiske, John. *Reading the Popular.* Boston: Unwin Hyman, 1989.

Garber, Marjorie. *Vested Interests: Cross-Dressing and Cultural Anxiety.* New York: Routledge, 1992.

Merck, Mandy. *Perversions: Deviant Readings by Mandy Merck.* London: Virago, 1993.

Meyer, Moe. "Introduction: Reclaiming the Discourse of Camp." In *The Politics and Poetics of Camp.* London: Routledge, 1994. 1–22.

O'Neill, John. *Five Bodies: The Human Shape of Modern Society.* Ithaca, N.Y.: Cornell University Press, 1985.

Ouimette, Victor. *Reason Aflame: Unamuno and the Heroic Will.* New Haven: Yale University Press, 1974.

Parker, Richard G. *Bodies, Pleasures, and Passions: Sexual Culture in Contemporary Brazil.* Boston: Beacon, 1991.

Ross, Andrew. "Uses of Camp." *Yale Journal of Criticism* 2.1 (fall 1988): 1–24.

Schwichtenberg, Cathy. Introduction. *The Madonna Connection: Representational Politics, Subcultural Identities, and Cultural Theory.* Boulder, Colo.: Westview Press, 1993.

Sontag, Susan. "Notes on 'Camp.'" In *Against Interpretation and Other Essays.* 1966. New York: Anchor, 1990. 275–292.

Travers, Andrew. "An Essay on Self and Camp." *Theory, Culture, and Society* 10 (1993): 127–143.

Walters, Suzanna Danuta. *Material Girls: Making Sense of Feminist Cultural Theory.* Berkeley and Los Angeles: University of California Press, 1995.

Weil, Kari. *Androgyny and the Denial of Difference.* Charlottesville: University Press of Virginia, 1992.

Westmoreland, Maurice. "Camp in the Works of Luis Zapata." *Modern Language Studies* 25.2 (spring 1995): 45–59.

Zapata, Luis. *Adonis García, A Picaresque Novel.* Trans. Edward A. Lacey. San Francisco: Gay Sunshine Press, 1981.

———. *Las aventuras, desventuras y sueños de Adonis García, el vampiro de la colonia Roma.* Mexico City: Editorial Grijalbo, 1979.

———. *En jirones.* Mexico City: Editorial Posada, 1985.

———. *La hermana secreta de Angélica María.* Mexico City: Cal y Arena, 1989.

———. *¿Por qué mejor no nos vamos?* Mexico City: Cal y Arena, 1992.

 **SIX**

From "Infernal
Realms of
Delinquency" to
Cozy Cabañas in
Cuernavaca: José
Joaquín Blanco's
Visions of
Homosexuality

The only thing that can console one for
being poor is extravagance.
—Oscar Wilde, *A Few Maxims for the
Instruction of the Over-Educated*

There is a popular expression in Spanish that goes something like "Nadie es
profeta en su tierra" (No one is a prophet in his or her homeland). That is
to say, one's words and opinions are heeded more seriously and given greater
credence elsewhere than in one's own land or culture. At the risk of making
this writer sound too apocalyptic or his ideas somehow divinely inspired, it
seems possible to conclude that José Joaquín Blanco's 1979 essay entitled "Ojos
que da pánico soñar" ("Eyes I Dare Not Meet in Dreams") holds a certain
prophetic quality. This is particularly evident when the essay is considered
in the context of two of his subsequent novels, *Las púberes canéforas* (The
pubescent nymphs) (1983) and *Mátame y verás* (Just kill me and you'll see)
(1994). The potential dangers of democratic tolerance and economic assimilation into the consumer mainstream of which he warns the "dear reader" at the
end of the 1970s have all but taken hold and become the "norm" of everyday
life a short fifteen years later.

Following Blanco's own words, in a revolutionary novel such as *Las aven-*

*turas, desventuras y sueños de Adonis García, el vampiro de la colonia Roma
(Adonis García: A Picaresque Novel)* (1979), an object of derision and carica-
ture—a gay male hustler—was turned instead into a serious, honest, joyful
subject of his own narrative story (Blanco 1990, 190). But the novel also represented the effervescence and exalted hopes of an era in which gay men and
lesbians in Mexico poured out into the streets, identifying themselves publicly
for the first time as individuals as well as members of gay groups and organizations. With the appearance of the vampire, an entirely subterranean city was
brought to light and celebrated with true joy for the radically different utopian
possibilities it offered. As Juan Carlos Bautista recalls, the 1970s were "años de
destape, de salidas masivas del clóset" (the explosive years of social awakening, of massive numbers of people coming out of the closet) (1993, 65). Yet in
1979, while standing up and being counted as one of the first critics to praise
the virtues, both aesthetic and political, of Zapata's literary character as well
as the liberation of homosexuals in the streets, Blanco nonetheless sounded
a cautious note. In his essay, originally published in the Saturday supplement
of the newspaper *unomásuno*, he wrote of the possible future implications of
such works and acts as those witnessed over the preceding several years. Ad-
dressing himself to middle-class gays in particular, since it is among them that
buying power has been greatest and tolerance by mass-consumer society has
made inroads more easily, Blanco warned of giving up the struggle to survive
and the obligation to invent a way of life by giving in to the promises of economic democracy as a tragedy to be avoided at all costs (1991; 291, 293). For
Blanco, the emerging policy of tolerating difference might serve to reinforce
class privilege and political conformity, thereby eliding radical politics and
subversive sexuality into just another "lifestyle choice" in the big city. He fore-
saw freedom from overt persecution as a right made available only to *some*
who would be required, in turn, to give up any real sense of difference in exchange for being allowed to coexist along with all other consumers (the one
identity shared by all involved). He predicted: "the system will try to tame
us by means of a deal: in return for our abandoning the radical possibility
of totally dropping out and ceasing any cooperation with the system, we'll be
given due respect and protection by the police, and the mass media will campaign for us to be respected in our jobs and in daily life, just as in the United
States, until we have been rendered happy and harmless" (1991, 292). He envisioned a shift from the feared gaze of the "eyes dare not met in dreams" to

a society politely looking the other way. As a legacy of that headier era, one looked back upon with a certain amount of nostalgia ten years later, from the vantage point of what he calls "estos tiempos oscurecidos" (these darkened and confused times) (1990, 193), *Adonis García* represents for Blanco a crucial marker. It signals "la feliz culminación de otra lucha, la ideológica, por liberar la vida amorosa de las viejas persecuciones [y] prejuicios" (the felicitous end of another battle, an ideological one, to liberate one's love life from age-old persecutions and prejudices) (1990, 191). Despite the desire to avoid apocalyptic prophecy, the implication of such an imminent break is there; an era has reached its limits, and changes are about to occur.

Las púberes canéforas, published a scant four years later, narrates the beginnings of skepticism and disenchantment of the 1980s, a time of social transition as well as the immediate proving ground for Blanco's earlier conjectures. The economic upheavals in the oil market (and their almost immediate consequences for consumers), the demythification of the façade of national progress, the advent of AIDS as a specter now visible on the horizon of the celebrated subterranean city and its inhabitants,[1] and what Sara Sefchovich has called "la disneyzación" (227) of Mexican culture, turning Disney-style theme parks and amusement centers (as well as cultural tourism) into the guiding icons of leisure-time diversion for the newly rich, practically extinguished the middle classes along with their hopes for the tolerant, if not supportive, coexistence of all of their members. Both old and new right-wing conservatives lashed out against homosexuals who ostensibly threatened the progress of the West with their "fiebre rosa," or pink fever, as AIDS was initially referred to in the press. As Ignacio Rubio Carriquiriborde writes, "Un virus logró catalizar rencores y enfrentar en un nuevo terreno a viejos enemigos" (A virus managed to catalyze animosities and brought old enemies face to face on new ground) (53). A wave of persecution against homosexuals swept through Mexico once again, stopped (at least temporarily) only by the devastating earthquake in September of 1985. Some have characterized this decade as composed of two halves: the first five years are the party and the second five are "la cruda," or the hangover (Bautista 65). In these terms, Blanco's 1983 novel falls squarely within the time of revelry, albeit already tinged with some measure of uncertainty, and is a chronicle of the insurgent violence in the metropolis, of a utopian world upon which the shadows of doubt and disbelief are beginning to fall. Yet we also find at the core of the text a sustained debate of sorts on the representations of homosexuality in life and in art, and therefore a tacit refusal to give in to phantoms, persecution, ingenuous celebration, or even social invisibility. Blanco's characters represent a counterpoint to one another, a tension between the desire to explore homosexuality and the limits placed on such desires whether by means of physical violence or psychological repression. The big question, however, is that of "difference" or, as Ruiz Esparza puts it, the opposition between "lo homosexual como ansia de participación" (homosexuality as the burning desire to participate) and "la homosexualidad como estrategia de rebeldía" (homosexuality as a strategy of rebellion) (247). By engaging this dilemma as the heart of the narrative, Blanco's novel forms a point of transition between the stimulus of liberation and the necessity of self-examination.

The characters Guillermo, La Gorda (the fat woman; the fat queen), Felipe, Analía, and Claudia are all products of a society that seems to consume them. On the one hand, we have Felipe, eighteen-year-old son of blue-collar parents, a *chichifo* (gay male prostitute) enthralled by the ideas of social mobility, expensive clothing, physical attractiveness, and all sorts of technology, who nevertheless, without missing a beat, makes plans to set up house with a female prostitute, Analía, as a front for a free relationship and a chance to get ahead in life. Felipe leaves his lover/client Guillermo for Analía, who works out of the top floor of a fleabag hotel but who shares Felipe's dreams of living in a new apartment in a building with an elevator, buying a car, and acquiring all the mechanical gadgets they have seen advertised on television and in the movies. Yet this dream must be placed in the context of the possibilities offered by the voracious city they inhabit; long before we read their present stories — in fact, in the first chapter — Analía's roommate Claudia is killed and Felipe is kidnapped and beaten by two men in a car who dump him by the side of the highway on the outskirts of town. They leave him for dead, but his ingenuity and will to live win out. This opening episode does not bode well for their plans, although both manage to survive in spite of the violence that surrounds them. Toward the end of the novel, Felipe is raffled off as a prize at a friend's private party to spend the evening with Irene, his lover Guillermo's ex-wife. In other words, this rigged contest has made the professedly liberal ex-spouses rivals for the affections of the *chichifo*. It is their host's revenge on their masquerade of tolerance, and we are left to imagine what occurs between them. Given the tone established by the first chapter, what is declared by day does not necessarily coincide with what is practiced by night. The human lottery is merely one moment of confrontation and challenge; other skirmishes take place in and around the city on a daily basis.

On the other hand, there is Guillermo, a forty-year-old minor bureaucrat who aspires to be a writer but is unable to get his thoughts down on paper in any form. He has spent years planning books he cannot write. Bored by his mediocre job and by the solitude he suffers as a middle-aged gay man, Guillermo entertains himself and makes his life bearable by composing stories (mostly to himself). So literature becomes, for him, an alternative to life. Felipe and his material dreams are the fuel for Guillermo's narratives, but he criticizes their vulgarity at the same time. Guillermo thinks of young men as slaves to cheap sensuality and to the middle class's idealization of the body as the temple of consumer culture, as commercialized objects made into fetishes for men in their forties ardently to desire. His intellectual analysis of this situation does not preclude him from playing out the very role he claims to despise.

Despite Guillermo's own desperate passion for Felipe—an exemplary representative of "esa sexualidad artificial y lustrosa que pese a todos sus rollos metafísicos era lo que lo prendía" (that artificial glossy sexuality which in spite of all his metaphysical babbling was what turned him on) (41)—his criticism of society's youth cult continues. As Guillermo yearns to polish his linguistic ability and his writing, making them increasingly glossy and artificial in their own right, he feels the pull of a similar drive for perfection imposed on physical relationships. His thoughts regarding "ese ideal del coito homosexual como encuentro de semidioses basketbolistas reluciendo músculos de estreno" (that ideal of homosexual coitus as a meeting between basketball-playing demigods showing off their gleaming new muscles) (40) or "ser supermanes en el colchón" (being supermen in bed) (41) appear in the text side by side with a poem by Spanish Baroque writer and aesthetic perfectionist Francisco de Quevedo, as if to make Guillermo's and Quevedo's quests for an expressive ideal indistinguishable from one another. From the media, Felipe has learned to value prices, progress (the jewels in the crown of the modern city are its high-rises and skyscrapers, for example), and glitzy U.S. culture. But Guillermo constantly admonishes him to forget such material things a bit and cultivate his intellect instead. The recalcitrant Felipe rejects the suggestion to "leer un poco" (read a little) (46), in favor of the utopian images fed to him through popular music, foreign films, publicity posters, and slick television commercials. If Felipe is the perfect example of a homosexuality of participation (Ruiz Esparza 247), then Guillermo represents the aestheticizing of homosexuality into (some kind of perfect) discourse, or "[una] diferencia [política y sexual] . . . que se convierte en escritura" ([a political and sexual] difference . . . that becomes a written text) (Ruiz Esparza 233). But one might ask how this can be reconciled with what the narrator reveals to us about Guillermo's greatest wish (aside from writing his novel, which increasingly seems to come in second): "no quería ya hacer otra cosa en su puta vida que coger con Felipe, coger con Felipe y coger con Felipe" (he no longer wanted to do anything in this shitty life but fuck with Felipe, fuck with Felipe, and fuck with Felipe) (53). For Guillermo, theory and practice—actual physical contact versus purified expressions of sentiment—are two lines that never intersect. One must give way to the other.

Baroque in his own way, the character La Gorda is a less than stellar dentist prone to excesses of pain and pleasure, drinking companion and sometime confidant of Guillermo, and eternal seeker of "the truth" behind all masks. For him, this "truth" is the object of too much artifice and not enough human passion and desire. He abhors the false pretensions of Guillermo and proposes an alternative: "Entre más crudas, incluso más obscenas, las cosas [son] menos mentirosas" (The more coarse, even obscene, things are, the more honest) (42). Even though he is approximately the same age as Guillermo and ostensibly dedicates a good number of hours every day to bodybuilding, La Gorda feels old among young men such as Felipe who don't seem interested in him anymore. Instead, the novel is replete with passages in which the dentist recounts in minute detail his adolescent adventures with lower-class Indians, who epitomize his ideal of rustic or primitive sexuality. As they age, and as the effects of poverty and malnutrition set in, they lose favor in his eyes. But in their (and his) youth, he finds them physically attractive to the point of being irresistible. Such a romanticized image of "native" sensuality reinforces the divisions of social class: La Gorda finds "decent," white, monied families to be held back by norms, laws, and the Christian concept of "virtue" (58), while "la gente que está abajo . . . como está más cerca del diablo y de los animales" (people from down in the lower classes . . . are like closer to the devil and to the animals) (58). The poor cannot be receptacles of "decency," an ideal reserved for the wealthy, so they are made to embody instead some diabolically attractive "natural" and unrestricted sexuality. La Gorda tells us that, even as a child, he never felt afraid to let people know he was gay and that it didn't seem to be something to be ashamed of, whereas his father's being a senator for the PRI (Partido Revolucionario Institucional, the country's official political party for most of the twentieth century) was indeed a shameful fact to be kept hidden (56). In this he is quite unlike Guillermo, who has even been married, perhaps in acquiescence to societal pressure or to his own repression.

Both as a child and later as an adult, La Gorda loves to chat, invent stories, and imagine vivid scenes of physical assault, abduction, capture, and rape in which the protagonists are always himself and various groups of Indians. These eroticized adventures culminate in orgies "a lo natural" (spontaneous, naked, without pretense, in the natural outdoors) (60). Guillermo builds barriers between language (artificial forms of expression) and physical acts (incapable of expression; to be enjoyed but not recounted in words); La Gorda fuses the two into a frenzy of (oral) carnality. For him, sexuality is both aggression and transgression; it is an antidote to Guillermo's textual impotence and, as we have said before, a strategy of rebellion (Ruiz Esparza 247), much as his black-market sales of electronic equipment fly in the face of official policy (at least to some extent, although during the 1980s *la fayuca,* or contraband, especially in technology, flourished while the federal government "tolerantly" looked the other way). Therefore, the "law"—what is written down—does not interrupt his activities but instead reinforces their potential for retelling, replete with reinvented details in each new version.

According to Felipe, Guillermo feels the same lust for men as he does but refuses to acknowledge it in material terms. It is a conclusion actually contradicted by the omniscient narrator, but of this Felipe is unaware. Instead, Guillermo lives a liberal middle-class existence, in civilized reconciliation with his ex-wife (who claims she finds homosexuals the perfect objects of "tolerant" admiration, compassion, and curiosity [135]) and in search of exalted emotions put into words and expressions of love. He even takes an elegant fountain pen and writes a sonnet about love and beauty by Spanish poet Luis de Góngora on the back of a nude photograph of Felipe. It would appear that neither is sufficient without the other, or that "nature" lacks the stamp of approval of "art": the "natural" is improved by the artifice of writing, and the written word finds its referent in the flesh of (a particular) youth. The private gathering near the end of the novel reflects the very same dilemma. Mixing together in one extravagantly campy mansion classical music, talented performers, pianists, art collectors, and other examples of the supposed confluence of high art and gay "sensibility," the gathering places Felipe's bare body on display as well. This is true in a literal sense because he is part of the fixed raffle already mentioned, but a Mr. Gay Hercules '82 competition also takes place, in which youthful male flesh is celebrated just as enthusiastically as "high art" has been up until then. Losing the object of his affection to his wife, Guillermo takes his leave of the celebration. The veneer of tolerance has been scratched. En route home, he asks himself why one should bother to elevate the deepest of sentiments to a level of lyricism and ecstasy when they always fall back into what they "really" are — "groseros, vulgares, confusos, abrumadores" (rude, coarse, confused, overwhelming) (142). Confusion and awe are not necessarily negatives, but "baseness" and "vulgarity" would deny any validity to these experiences. His refined assimilation into family life (a masquerade now ended) and a "decent" job (repetitive and boring) has never placed him farther from Felipe's sexuality in the flesh as now. Confusion reigns in his reaction, it is true, but what he refers to as the "vulgar" is also just what he celebrates in Felipe's sexuality.

Ultimately, it is the public bathhouses, once a refuge for homosexuals excluded from meeting almost everywhere else and later a space of unbridled revelry, that symbolize the difference in attitude between Guillermo and La Gorda. They also offer the venue for the dentist's demise — or final rebellion, depending on one's point of view. Guillermo finds "Los Baños Jáuregui" (the Jauregui Baths) squalid and repulsive, a place unworthy of gay men who, in his opinion, should aspire to ennoble their lives rather than meeting in hidden and "sórdidos chiqueros" (squalid pigsties) (143) like the steam rooms. For him, encounters of the flesh should be ceremonious and aesthetically charged, capable of evoking refined passions and not base desires. (Ironically, he seeks the latter in Felipe, whose photographed image he later attempts to endow with "nobility" by subtitling it with Góngora's love sonnet.)

Conversely, La Gorda defends the transgressive potential of these public-yet-private meeting places as his only conceivable home turf: "No había escogido esa perra vida, decía, para convertirla en miembro de los coros angelicales, sino precisamente por lo que tenía de perra. . . . [Los baños eran] los reinos infernales de la delincuencia, de la violencia y del desorden" (He hadn't chosen this rotten life, he said, in order to change it into another member of the choirs of angels, but rather precisely for how rotten it was. . . . [The baths were] the infernal realms of delinquency, of violence, and of chaos) (143). Far from being inhabited by the barely material "púberes canéforas" of the title, a reference to virginal maidens at the service of the goddess Diana taken from a modernist poem by Nicaraguan Rubén Darío, for La Gorda the baths are the perfect spot to play up and act out the camp aspects of identity. The steam rooms defy the "cleanliness" of society by their promises of unbridled sexuality, limited only by the participants' decision to enter or not. In the stark contrasts between the poverty and decrepit façade of the colonial building where they are located and the bright packaging of the beauty products sold there to clients along-side neon-lit religious statues, he finds a personally affirming world of artifice and artificiality. La Gorda finds no contradiction whatsoever between the re-affirmation of the body in the health bar's "natural" products and the acts of sexual expression taking place in the other rooms.

Counting himself among the brave few who defy societal repression (144) by joining the ranks of those who frequent these steam-filled democratic equal-izers of young and old, fat and thin, ugly and attractive, La Gorda also notes the fact that bribery is needed to guarantee tolerance of these places by the au-thorities. He remarks that the sordidness of the building and its aging facilities is not a defect but an asset in that it keeps "decent" people out, and he revels in playing the role of antagonist to "decency." Like Jean Genet before him, if La Gorda is to be cast as a delinquent in the eyes of propriety, then he will play the role to the hilt; it is the only way for him to live honestly. He might sing the praises of the artificial—socially induced or produced signs of identity—but never of the falsely "respectable." La Gorda's willful surrender to the under-cover police agents waiting outside the Jáuregui Baths, forces he had paid off many times before, is an act of passion and political defiance to the very end. Since childhood, his ideal of virility has consisted of just such a show of force and violence. He recalls published episodes of aggression toward homosexuals accompanied in the media by dramatic photos and headlines, intermingled with stories such as one that includes the image of St. Sebastian's martyred body pierced by arrows. These memories lead him to feel "los espasmos del placer final" (the spasms of the final pleasure) (148), an allusion to sexuality and death in one fell swoop. He defies the law, which seeks to impose guilt and punishment on him; he has not fallen for the buyout of the "happy and harm-less" of which Blanco has warned, but seeks to revel in the ecstasy of confront-ing the agents of the law face to face. The decision is eminently political, as it is thoroughly personal: "en algún momento se llegaba al final de la calle, a la con-sumación de un destino" (at some moment one reaches the end of the road, the consummate end of a destiny) (148). When Guillermo has gone home after the party to pout over losing his muse Felipe to Irene, La Gorda faces up to the brutality of the city and assumes the ultimate stance of the delinquent. Such a forking of the paths after the festivities are over (whether in the mansion, the baths, or the nation for that matter), akin to the "hangover" of the latter part of the 1980s following the celebrations of gay culture earlier in the decade, appears to be a signal by Blanco of the need to make a deliberate choice. And the element of choice returns once again in the ceremonies of tolerance between Guillermo and Irene (parodied and criticized by the gay community as presented in the text) *or* the stand of La Gorda. To embark on both roads would be impossible. The novel closes with a decidedly brief section of two lines after the disquisitions of the bathhouse episodes, which cover nineteen pages. Taken from Quevedo, once again, the last entry reads: "Nada me desengaña; / el mundo me ha hechizado" (Nothing disillusions me; I'm bewitched by the world) (149). The "spell" of lived reality cannot be broken, even in its most threatening moments. Indeed, "the world," and not the abandonment of it, is the choice made here. Following on the heels of La Gorda's deliberate walk to an unmarked car in the company of representatives of the "law," these lines insinuate the capacity of radical politics to inspire art, since La Gorda writes his final chapter by carrying through this act, while Guillermo never pens a single line. The world is capable of keeping one under its thrall, even as it places obstacles in the middle of the road. The error, Blanco's text seems to suggest, is to run away and hide from the obstacles that challenge daily one's deepest convictions. Guillermo has been living vicariously through Felipe and the others he meets, even as he finds fault with their lives; but La Gorda has lived more "honestly" among the "coarse, even obscene" (see 42) realities of everyday life.

By 1994, the system appears to have struck its deal. After the 1987 stock market crash and the generalized electoral fraud of the 1988 elections, in which the official party (the PRI) imposed its will once again on Mexican voters in order to have Carlos Salinas de Gortari come out the winner, Salinas's six-year term (1988–94) consolidates, privatizes, and institutionalizes the substitution of consumer society and buying power for the politics practiced by La Gorda. The violent repression of homosexuals in the southern states of Oaxaca and Chiapas, and the equally disturbing deaths in Mexico City of medical personnel dedicated to the gay community's fight against AIDS, occur simultaneously alongside the widespread financial crises. But those who have "made it" are at the peak of their success — or are they? As a novel whose social vision is sharply satirical, *Mátame y verás* presents us with the growing anxiety to participate in the benefits of late-twentieth-century capitalism at its best (of course, in satire, at its worst). Forty-something investment banker Sergio Peña, father of two with the requisite house, country club membership, cars, and bankbook to prove his success, finds himself on the wrong end of divorce proceedings filed by his wife. The marriage has been dysfunctional for quite some time, but the Christmas holidays have precipitated the final rupture. He is obliged to hide out from her lawyers and her irate family until the two weeks of vacation are over and his own attorney can plan a counterattack. A defeated example of the modern Mexican dream, he takes refuge in student neighborhoods around the university where he will not be recognized and where he can afford to pay — his credit is the first casualty in their war. His newfound poverty and power-lessness create a distance from which Sergio can mull over the road he has taken to reach such a point. The economic orgy of the first part of his life is confronted with the self-reflexive part of the second.

Once again, as it was in *Las púberes canéforas* from the first scene of Felipe's kidnapping, the city is presented as both friend and foe, consoler and aggressor, to inhabitants such as Sergio. He can think of only one way out of his current misery and loss of identity: "Largarse de la Ciudad de México a como diera lugar" (Get out of Mexico City, however possible) (11). But this is easier said than done, given the congestion of the streets as well as the scarcity of his financial resources. Amid the apocalyptic vision of air pollution, traffic jams, and the fever of gift buying as if there were no tomorrow, Sergio runs into a familiar figure loaded down with elegant packages. Juan Jácome, better known as Juanito to his former college classmates, is the picture of conspicuous consumption: "un dandy el cabrón como envuelto para regalo él mismo, rozagante, relajado, perfumado, como nuevecito, con ropa sport de firma, su reloj ahí como que no quería la cosa, nomás para que hiciera juego con dos que tres anillazos" (The bastard looked like a real dandy, as if he himself were gift-wrapped, splendid, relaxed, perfumed, like just-out-of-the package brand new, with designer sport clothes, his watch sitting there like he really didn't want to wear it but put it on just to match the two or three huge rings he was wearing) (15). Pointedly asking whether the reader remembers him from their university years, and thereby bringing him or her into direct contact with the text, Sergio takes no chances and clarifies the connection: "Ese, el putito — qué putito ni qué putito: putazo" (That guy, the little fag—what do I mean little fag: the big fag) (16) who was always sent on errands, insulted until he was reduced to tears, exploited economically, and abused in every way possible by the students with whom he (inexplicably?) wanted to socialize. Here is the point at which Blanco steps in to even the score, however. While, in those days, Sergio had long been the great hope for the future, with his talent for making long-shot investments pay off and his marriage to a beautiful, sexually liberated young woman from a good family, Juanito (even twenty-two years later, as an adult, Sergio uses the childish nickname) quit school and was cut off from everyone else once they married and were set in their comfortable urban prosperity. In middle age, the situation has been reversed and Juanito, anxious emulator of his straight classmates who always seemed to desire nothing more than to be part of the crowd, prospers while Sergio begs for a place to go for the holidays. No longer the object of scorn—"Walk like a man!" is the advice Sergio remembers giving him—Juanito has bought his way into decency and respectability in the eyes of Peña. His material success has made him "harmless." There is no hesitation whatsoever in Sergio's effusive greeting, a fact that surprises Juanito but which is explained and justified to himself by an internal monologue: "a los dieciocho años se preocupa uno demasiado por mantener distancias, a los cuarenta, y jodido, te vale madres que un puto te salude a gritos y se te lance a los brazos en plena calle" (at eighteen one worries too much about keeping a distance, at forty, and all screwed up, you don't give a damn if a fag greets you in a loud voice and throws himself into your arms in the middle of the street) (16). After all, Juanito has a distinguished air about him (even if has the same walk, Sergio notes), his arms are full of expensive purchases, and Sergio is searching desperately for a temporary way out of his misery. These ironies are played out through the rest of the novel, with Juanito functioning as the mirror in which Sergio examines his own life—an interesting reversal (dare I say "inversion"?) of models.

Typing on the keyboard of his laptop computer, as any successful businessman of the 1990s might, Sergio records his recollections of episodes from the past in a sort of diary for posterity (and for himself); he writes, "inicié este pormenorizado informe, a ver si algún día llego a comprenderme yo mismo" (I started this detailed report to see if someday I'll manage to understand myself) (51). His silence of so many years—a sort of closet aspect to his life—is broken by the recent marital rupture, which forces him to scrutinize the past.

In the process, he reviews the multitude of changes that have taken place in his life, yet we should not lose sight of the fact that his story, at least until it is printed up in hard copy, is a virtual one: it belongs to the glowing blue computer screen alone. The first episode he recalls is the matter-of-fact sexual encounter with Juanito on a religious retreat, and his rejection of any further intimacy; he claims that he only used Juanito as an escape valve for the frustration created by societal prohibition of physical relations with "decent" young women. Their encounter has no "name"; Sergio does not imbue it with any further meaning and, in a way, "blames it" on Carmela for not giving in to his desires. And he reviews other moments, ending by describing the "Marido Ejemplar" (Exemplary Husband) he has been up until a few days earlier when the divorce papers were filed. In both instances, what is revealed is a "pact" with society: Sergio is not to be considered gay as long as there are no further encounters between himself and Juanito, and the perfect husband is a category of mutual tolerance by tacit agreement (both husband and wife can cheat as long as neither openly accuses the other of any wrongdoing).

Sergio is eager to take on the novel adventure of spending the Christmas holidays "con una tribu de maricones" (with a whole tribe of fags) (24) as he calls Juanito and his friends, embarking on a journey into a limbo from which he can attempt to sort out his current situation. He assumes the challenge not as "himself," but in the guise of someone temporarily divested of his "real" identity; he accepts Juanito's invitation to go "de incognito" (on the sly; incognito) (24), or in disguise, as it were. Is it age that makes him more tolerant of his companions, or his lack of finances and the temptation of a vacation cottage? There are indications in the text that the latter is at work here, given the fact that Peña still worries, before he agrees to join them, about how politically militant, obvious, and visible his companions will be so as not to be confused with them. His "tolerance" stems from selfishness, and from the belief that Juanito has learned to "blend in." It is certainly ironic that Peña wants homosexuals to dissolve into the consumer ranks, while he wishes to maintain a distance from them so as not to be identified by others as a gay man. He decides not to shave before meeting his traveling companions, since, in his opinion, a neat appearance and clean-shaven face are the visible marks of homosexual identity. His host is careful to clarify that the holiday getaway is for purposes of relaxation only, not for sexual politics of any kind: "[Somos] unas locas de lo más pacíficas, a estas edades ya pasó la guerra" ([We're] the most peaceful bunch of queens [you can imagine], at this age the war is over) (924). Although he (paradoxically) criticizes the students in his boardinghouse for their obsession with material success, Sergio is more than willing to share the benefits of Juanito's economic status, which reflects an adoration of the very same values by which he himself has lived. They have at least one thing in common that can be named: an interest in upward mobility.

In a play on the phrase "ship of fools" (*locos*), Sergio refers to Juanito's automobile as "la nave de las *locas*" or the ship of queens (26). The five members of the crew, then, are Juanito himself; Sergio; middle-aged bodybuilder Rubén (a figure vaguely reminiscent of La Gorda, but only as far as his worship of the human body goes); intellectual, movie addict, ardent pursuer of proletarian lovers, and marijuana devotee *el Jirafón* (the giant giraffe); and Aníbal, a delicately beautiful young student of tourism who aspires to a career in show business and idolizes his lover Juanito. While Peña mulls over the suspicion that the four are trying to force him into the role of voyeur and get him involved somehow in their sexual activities, a fantasy of the wounded *macho* who finds no woman around who might be irresistibly drawn to him and him alone, Juanito and his friends fall into an equally stereotypical judgment of the newcomer. Upon arriving at the cabaña in the tiny town of San Isidro near the upscale town of Cuernavaca, and being welcomed with admiration and adoration by their neighbors, Sergio offers to prepare dinner for them all. Rubén concludes with great sarcasm that a straight man, by "nature" and talent unable to cook, will make them eat boiled rice, a fear put to rest with pride by the gourmet abilities of the volunteer chef. Over time, each side debunks many of the myths created and perpetuated by the other. For instance, Sergio's homogenization of gay men into one indistinguishable mass is contradicted by those present at the retreat. Aníbal has found a longed-for sense of security and stability in his upwardly mobile lover Juanito, but Rubén cruises the local bars in search of adventure, never content to remain with the same old crowd but lamenting that "escasea la carne fresca" (fresh meat is hard to find) (45). For his part, Juanito defends the pleasures of being free from the slavery of marriage and family in the traditional sense—what he sees as Sergio's curse— and the idea that instead "ellos inventaban cada día su familia entre puros extraños" (they could [re]invent their family every day among perfect strangers) (45), much as has taken place during this very gathering of holiday celebrants. Although he has already emphasized the relaxed tone of the people involved,

Juanito continues to maintain the crucial importance of one point. He firmly believes that all gay men should stick together, in spite of any possible differences of opinion, to keep from fragmenting or rupturing the community as a whole as a result of fights among themselves. The narrator (Sergio) tells the reader this succinctly in the following terms: "la liberación gay es su religión" (gay liberation is his religion) (45). But there are no disquisitions and no harangues: politics and activism do not take the form expected by Sergio. In fact, there is a general sense of good humor, acceptance, and enjoyment that is envied by Peña, who has lost the ability to free himself from the constraints of being "mature" and "serious" (44). Evidently, for him at least, being an adult excludes humor or joy of any sort, and the pleasures of sex for that matter, and the carnivalesque atmosphere of the cabaña is a signal to him that gay men take life too lightly. (First, he worries about the visibility of their politics, then he is preoccupied that they don't take politics seriously enough.) The theatrics and performances of the four friends, along with a liberal dose of alcohol, do finally convince Sergio that one *can* be an adult without sacrificing a passionate delight in the pleasures of life. Yet some vestige of doubt always seems to linger in his comments about their "lifestyle," an echo of the language used in the liberal press in its "tolerant" reporting of alternative experiences. Without the liquor, and outside the cabaña, Sergio seems less convinced.

A curious parallel is set up between Rubén's inebriated confession and Sergio's reconstructed personal story, leading to the denouement of a Christmas masquerade ball as the revelation of the theatricality of all such social rituals and identities. Rubén has defied any matrimonial union with another man as a mere parody of heterosexual couples, at least until he runs into César. The tragic ending to their love story comes, however, when César loses his fight against cancer, after first dropping out of sight so as to leave behind only the memory of a perfect physical appearance. He wants to linger in the memory of his lover rather than be pitied or consoled. Rubén is left to examine and reexamine the feeling of having fallen in love with the alluring and seductive countenance of death itself in the guise of a young man cut down in the prime of life showing no external signs of what he suffers. The paradox of an alluring image of death obsesses Rubén. Sergio and his wife Carmela are similarly linked by physical attraction (at least initially) but, in their case, the wild adolescent freedom of constantly testing the limits of patriarchal power (the rule of her father) plays a central role in the demise of their relationship once Sergio settles into a comfortable routine and she wants to continue social climbing. What sets him back is his dark skin—he refers to himself as "étnico y aztecoide" (ethnic-looking and Aztecoide) (69)—which, during their younger days, was a mark of Carmela's social defiance in the eyes of her family. In Mexican society's hierarchy of skin tones, Sergio's darkness would not be an asset to him. Now, Sergio has become like the stigma of an unremovable tattoo. Carmela has come to her senses. Besides, the fashion of marrying "down" into a more evidently indigenous ethnic group, a fad of the 1960s, is no longer chic. Carmela conveniently falls in love with a customs agent, a younger version of Sergio, and revels in the one additional difference between them: his pale white skin.

The dreams of Rubén and César are broken only by the latter's sudden illness, and the moments between them are frozen in time; those of Carmela and Sergio are torn apart by daily boredom, emotional distance, and the process of aging itself, which has reached a critical moment in their lives. So the so-called copy—a gay couple uniting "in parody of" a straight couple—proves to be more "genuine" than the original, except, of course, for the fact that César and Rubén are locked into an eternal image of youth whereas Sergio and Carmela have seen that image fade over the last twenty-two years. Carmela tries to recapture some shadow of the past by exchanging her husband for a younger man; Sergio attempts to resuscitate the body of an eighteen-year-old Carmela in the arms of a youthful prostitute (41). Rubén worships the art of bodybuilding and the cult of fitness centers as the twentieth century's new temples to the god of youth—in this instance, the motivation is to be ready to reunite with César after death, both in the very same shape they were in when they parted.

The campy appearance of a group of transvestite performers on a holiday excursion lounging around the swimming pool of a local inn creates a situation that becomes a dress rehearsal for their Christmas Eve celebration. Without their makeup, wigs, jewelry, or evening clothes, the visitors look to Sergio like "sapos a la luz del sol, esperando la luna de las princesas" (toads in the sunlight, waiting for the moon [to turn them into] princesses) (99). In point of fact, they are represented by the narrator as similar to Mexican society in general, which takes on a different guise each time it dresses up as something (someone?) else. They appropriate the appearance of the other in mocking exaggeration, but in the light of day enjoy the benefits of leisure time while exposing their "real" faces to the sun. While constantly playing up his so-called seriousness about assuming the responsibilities of middle age, family life, and high-pressure job—"a mis cuarenta años confío en valores más sólidos, más seguros" (at forty I put my trust in more solid, more secure values) (107) he repeats throughout the novel, albeit with a tone of constantly diminishing conviction—Sergio's participation in the collective festivities seals his pact with a vision of all social identity as disguise and masquerade. This, of course, includes his own. Freed from everyday routine during this parenthesis in his daily life, "se siente dispuesto a aceptar las cosas diferentes o extrañas; el mundo se vuelve menos estricto" (one feels predisposed to accept things that are different or strange; the world becomes less strict) (131) and his affection for his companions grows. Nevertheless, he still maintains the opinion that deep down inside there is a barrier between them that can never be overcome: "uno nunca entiende a los putos" (one never really understands fags) (138). Sergio seems to signal that there is some fundamental difference between himself and the others. After removing the outer layers of appearance, there is an unapproachable core. In ironic counterpoint, Juanito echoes a similar vision of straight men when he concludes that "los heteros . . . no tienen remedio" (heterosexuals . . . they're hopeless) (141). Comprehension and camaraderie seem to Sergio like two different spheres. So even this time spent together will create no lasting bond. But instead of going to bed and hiding under the covers for two weeks until the familial storm blows over—his first reaction to their gatherings—Sergio ventures out to join the party filled with carefully planned stages of merriment hosted by Juanito. All those present have agreed to one thing, to a greater or lesser degree, and that is the need to poke fun at life and take pleasure in doing so. The single exception, AIDS, "la palabra prohibida" (the banned word) (131), is mentioned but once, creating an air of tension until even this is dissipated by a series of jokes by Juanito and el Jirafón. The artificial space of limbo is maintained; the rest of the world is staved off, at least within the walls of the cabaña. Or so it seems. This campy atmosphere constantly measures its distance from the so-called "outside" (from where it ravages and plunders for its own encoded identities), making of Juanito's cabaña a larger-than-life-size closet from which these gay men emerge at the end of each stay. The surrounding town welcomes the group with open arms in terms that suggest a traveling carnival. Each holiday, and during the summer months, they grace the hamlet with their extravagant presence, seduce the locals with their chatter and theatrical dress, then return to the city to earn enough for the next round.

In the surprise presentation they have reserved for Sergio, Rubén, Juanito,

Aníbal, and el Jirafón don elaborate costumes and begin a pageant of television and movie stars. The members of the group parody the popular images
of heroes and heroines, exaggerating their physical characteristics and reveling
in being identified with their most famous (and recognizable) roles. Among
these examples of "marginales y perdedores" (marginal losers) (133) as he
refers to both the actors and their idols, Sergio finally admits to himself that he
feels more at home than he did in the strained and ultimately sad company of
his other family. He concludes that the Christmas holidays have always been
empty performances with Carmela and their children, so at least Juanito and
his companions have allowed Sergio the chance to embrace such a scenario
openly as an act. Left alone to "be himself," "feliz en ese momento de ser un
freak más, con mis propias locuras" (for the moment happy to be just another
freak, with my own crazy ideas) (133), Sergio gets caught up in the presentation of their *zarzuela* (musical comedy operetta). During this production of
stars, the glittering masks over the faces of the actors are no more (or less) of a
masquerade than his role as father and husband to Carmela and their children.
(The fact that it is a role is emphasized by the easy replacement of Sergio by
another suitor, the customs agent, who steps into his shoes overnight.) Sergio
has been harboring the fear all along that Juanito and the others will be overly
sentimental and *cursi* (corny, tacky, campy), yet he is the one who sings the
syrupy lyrics of a romantic ballad far into the night until no one can stand
his teary voice any longer. It is ironic that he calls this the performance of a
Latin lover (138), although its tone of flirtation recalls more Juanito's manner
of expression than Sergio's, at least in the opinion of the narrator. Peña tries,
with little success, to recover moments from the past, which appear only as
fleeting instants of nostalgia linked to lovers' names written in the sand, ocean
waves crashing on a beach, and similar stock-in-trade clichés. The return of his
paranoia, a dimension of his life from before this emotional and geographical
limbo, leads Sergio to accuse Juanito of broadcasting his sentimental serenade
via a cellular phone to Carmela. He finally is forced to repent for this accusation, but not before he becomes a centerpiece of their show.[2]

The novel, originally serialized in reader-friendly fragments in the Mexican magazine *Etcétera* between February and April 1994, ends with neither
apologies nor remorse on the part of any of the characters. On the contrary—
Juanito declares he has his life "in order" (111), is no longer servile to anyone
except seductive consumption, has been consecrated by the gods of (foreign)

culture by means of frequent trips to Europe, and defends his new consumer image as harboring no intrinsic evil. Rather, he finds a certain amount of perverse pleasure in the buying power that results from society's tolerant capitalist work ethic, because the money is there for him to spend as he sees fit. And this is where his politics lie: in the militancy of the marketplace, into whose hallowed halls (malls?) Juanito has gained entry at last. The orgy has moved from the streets into *Perisur* and other urban shopping centers of the supermodern variety. In place of the collective organization and common goals of the closet-emptying 1970s and early 1980s, Juanito exemplifies what Sefchovich sees currently as a translation of modernity into "el modo de vida . . . individualista, posesivo y ruidoso. . . . Cultura de tono fácil, de respuestas inmediatas . . . , de velocidad" (the lifestyle [that is] individualist, possessive, and sensationally loud. . . . Cheap culture, one with instant answers . . . , fast culture) (254). In spite of his in-laws' "old money," Sergio falls into exactly the same category as well. His financial success is due to the very same investment and business opportunities of which Juanito has taken equal advantage. The two are mirror images of each other, as are many in the crowded subway station into which these characters melt and disperse once again at the end of the narrative. They both blend back into the social fabric that has given them the chance to prosper.

But through such characters' worship at the altars of the "cathedrals of consumption" (Fiske 13), Blanco also offers a glimpse into the masquerade of the marketplace, which attempts to gloss over (tolerate) all political statements by turning them into elements of "style."[3] Commodities have become the icons of the modern for both Sergio and Juanito, and rituals of conspicuous consumption (during Christmas and New Year's, for example) are available to anyone with the right amount of cash or an open credit line, but the pleasure taken is ephemeral. It is not made equivalent in the text to the freedoms of university politics as nostalgically evoked by Sergio, or to the political skirmishes Juanito proclaims as something belonging only to the past of these now-tranquil (pacified? pacifist? pacific? [24]) homosexuals. (Yet it must be noted that both the political attitudes of the past and the lack of such overt commitment in the present are equally made the objects of satire by the narrative voice that alternates with Sergio's.)[4] The guerrilla tactics of the consumer as active agent, making sense of him- or herself as a subject by consuming objects of choice, as promoted by present-day theorists of popular culture such as Fiske, use as referents the subordinate (Fiske 7), the marginal, the dispossessed lower classes with little or no access to the systems of production either economically or ideologically. The economic power wielded by Juanito or Sergio (at least in his former incarnation as paterfamilias par excellence) bears no relation to such potential forces of erosion, but instead has everything to do with joining the seduction of (by) bourgeois values. If these acts blur many of the traces of difference among the characters on the superficial level — their appearance, speech, occupations, eating habits, sexual practices, etc. — the one visible sign of identity that is left is class. Despite the bitingly humorous tone of Blanco's satire of Mexican society through the shared obsessions of these individuals, the reader feels haunted by the words of La Gorda, who rejected the "angelic choirs" (143) of happy consumers in order to defend the so-called delinquency of difference. At the end of the road, that character found the hulking agents of the law; Juanito finds his own reflection in the dressing-room mirror and nothing to stop him from gazing at it to his heart's content.

Notes

1   Bautista cites 1985 specifically as "el año en que el sida (ese fantasma que venía co-lándose desde principios de la década y cada vez se volvía algo más concreto) hizo crisis en México" (the year in which AIDS [the phantom which had been infiltrat-ing its way into society since the beginning of the decade and kept getting more and more concrete] reached crisis proportions in Mexico) (65).

2   The use of the telephone for coaxing admissions of "truth" recalls a similar scene in Crowley's play *The Boys in the Band*. In the second of two acts, the group of gay friends who have congregated to celebrate a birthday challenge one another to each call the one person he truly believes he has loved. The eight gay men and the osten-sibly straight college roommate of one of them also recall the relationship between Juanito, his friends, and Sergio. The fight between Sergio and Rubén parallels as well the confrontation between Alan (the roommate from Georgetown) and Emory, the one member of the present group who refuses to dissimulate his sexuality.

3   One clear example of ideology-made-style is the chic clothing line whose label "1910 Revolution" is visible all over Mexico City on billboards, in store windows, and in fashion magazine advertisements. The stylishly baggy jeans and button-down denim "authentic worker" shirts being promoted have no connection whatsoever to the Mexican Revolution of 1910, but are used to suggest some vague radical "political" statement without, of course, being overtly political at all. Such state-

ments of appearance would seem to fall under the category of unintentional or high camp (see Isherwood, 110) which mimics or pokes fun at something taken much more seriously than it appears at first glance. It is obvious that an appropriation of the "1910 Revolution" reference on a shirt pocket or jeans label is intended both to identify with the power of the original reference (a moment of national social upheaval and charismatic leaders) and to transfer such power onto the wearer of currently stylish vestments, who, by a further act of transference, becomes invested with the residues of that same power — in economic, sexual, and social terms. (One need only look as far as Marlon Brando's cinematic portrayal of Emiliano Zapata to confirm the sexual power latent in the figure of that hero, or at least in its Anglo interpretation.)

4   Westmoreland points out the antithetical stance of camp to the politics of gay liberation (47). One must wonder whether this could possibly hold true for all cultures, however. In the case of Mexico, the ghetto *and* the closet both take on a variety of configurations, and their shifting characteristics make it difficult to place camp performance either inside or outside of either. The influence of gay tourists, and of Club Med–style getaway holidays to Ixtapa-Zihuatanejo, Cancún, Huatulco, and other resorts promoted by a variety of U.S. publications such as *The Advocate,* can also be seen in these categories, for example in the use of the slang term "internacionales" for gay men who take both active and passive roles in sex. In a broader sense, the term has taken on the meaning of "foreign" gay men or Mexican men who "copy" foreign attitudes and behaviors.

Works Cited

Bautista, Juan Carlos. "Pasión y muerte de la literatura gay: Luis Zapata." *Viceversa* 4 (mayo/junio 1993): 63–65.

Blanco, José Joaquín. "Eyes I Dare Not Meet in Dreams." Trans. Edward A. Lacey. In *Gay Roots: Twenty Years of Gay Sunshine.* Ed. Winston Leyland. San Francisco: Gay Sunshine Press, 1991. 291–296.

———. *Mátame y verás.* Mexico City: Era, 1994.

———. "Ojos que da pánico soñar." In *Función de medianoche: Ensayos de literatura cotidiana.* 1979. Mexico City: Era, 1981. 181–190.

———. *Las púberes canéforas.* 1983. Mexico City: Cal y Arena, 1991.

———. "Zapata: el vampiro en los años del SIDA." In *Las intensidades corrosivas.* Villahermosa, Mexico: Gobierno del Estado de Tabasco, 1990. 187–193.

Crowley, Mart. *The Boys in the Band.* New York: Farrar, Straus and Giroux, 1968.

Fiske, John. *Reading the Popular.* Boston: Unwin Hyman, 1989.

Isherwood, Christopher. *The World in the Evening.* New York: Random House, 1952.

Rubio Carriquiriborde, Ignacio. "El sida a los 17." *Mundo: Culturas y Gente* 68 (agosto 1994): 52–55.

Ruiz Esparza, Jorge. "Homotextualidad: La diferencia y la escritura." In *Coloquio internacional: Escritura y sexualidad en la literatura hispanoamericana.* Ed. Alain Sicard and Fernando Moreno. Madrid: Fundamentos, 1990. 233–252.

Sefchovich, Sara. *México: país de ideas, país de novelas: Una sociología de la literatura mexicana.* Mexico City: Grijalbo, 1987.

Westmoreland, Maurice. "Camp in the Works of Luis Zapata." *Modern Language Studies* 25.2 (spring 1995): 45–59.

Zapata, Luis. *Adonis García: A Picaresque Novel.* Trans. Edward A. Lacey. San Francisco: Gay Sunshine Press, 1981.

————. *Las aventuras, desventuras y sueños de Adonis García, el vampiro de la colonia Roma.* Mexico City: Grijalbo, 1979.

Index

violence, 6, 89, 98, 116, 120, 136; media and representation of, 70; sadomasochism and, 61–62, 72

Weiss, Andrea: on vampires and lesbians in film, 56n. 7

Zapata, Luis, 7–8, 9–10, 42–43, 44–45, 52, 107, 111; gay narrative subjects in works by, 125, 130n. 10, 133–134; representation of femininity in novels of, 117, 121–122

zones, 4, 12; of comfort, 11, 140; of danger, 3, 4, 6, 9, 12, 89, 100; of tolerance, 4, 5, 6, 9, 12, 12n. 1, 19, 53–54, 96, 100, 101. *See also* night, culture of; Pink Zone; tolerance

About the Author. Claudia Schaefer is a professor of Hispanic Literature and Culture at the University of Rochester. She is the author of numerous studies on twentieth-century Spain and Latin America, and her most recent book is *Textured Lives: Women, Art, and Representation in Modern Mexico,* published by the University of Arizona Press.